A. The Physical Setting

Yemen is by far the most fertile part of the Arabian peninsula, yet agriculture is a hard scrabble. There are two major regions: the smaller coastal region or Tihama and the more extensive mountainous highlands.

> The Tihama is a narrow, hot, humid semi-desert, an almost waterless strip that extends the entire seacoast from Maydi on the northern frontier with Saudi Arabia to the Bab al Mandab at the country's southern limits and occupies approximately 10% of the country[1]

These 20,300 sq. Km. miles are watered principally by seven major <u>wadis</u> carrying runoff from the highlands. Their waters seldom reach the sea and rarely flow throughout the year. The climate is oppressively tropical. Temperatures often reach 55 degrees c. and even in the cool season range into the 30's, humidity readings of 80% or more are not uncommon. Rainfall in the wetter areas of the Tihama only rarely exceeds 300 mm annually. Natural vegetation is sparse and the area is subject to severe windstorms and shifting sands.

Most of the rest of the country is mountainous. The mountains rise sharply from the Tihama and extend to the eastern escarpment, where one descends into the desolation of the Empty Quarter. While rainfall on the western and southern facings of the mountains around Taiz and Ibb reaches between 1,000 and 1,200 mm per annum, it decreases rapidly as one moves North and East. After crossing the range of mountains north of Ibb, the annual rainfall drops sharply and falls to 300 mm per year at Sanaa and to 200 mm per year at the Saudi Arabian border. On the eastern border of the country rain rarely falls. The interior of the country is marked by steep mountains, sharply eroded narrow wadis and dry highland plains. Much of the farming is carried out on terraced mountainsides, along the banks of wadis or on largely arid mountain plateaus. Temperatures in the mountain areas are a great improvement over Tihama with temperate summers and cool winters.

B. Historical Perspective

Settled agriculture has been practiced in Yemen for millennia and the evidence indicates that agricultural practices, production and productivity probably changed little over the thousand years before the overthrow of the Imam in 1962. During this period, crop production consisted primarily of grain crops, mostly sorghum and millet, plus limited varieties of fruit and vegetables such as grapes, apricots, almonds, figs, green onions, chives, hot peppers and white radishes. On rainfed land there was production of various legumes such as beans, peas, fenugreek, and lentils. Alfalfa was cultivated on irrigated land. Coffee and <u>qat</u> were introduced around the 15th century and cotton on a commercial scale in the mid-20th century. Coffee beans have been exported for a considerable period of time and most of the cotton was also exported. Livestock production consisted of cattle, goats, sheep, chickens, donkeys and camels. Livestock was used to provide food, transport and power for cultivation of crops and dung for fuel. Most agricultural production was consumed by the producer, though some small amounts were bartered or sold in the market. It was for the most part a self-contained economic society.

Nearly all Yemenis, certainly over 90%, were agriculturalists living off of the products of this farm system.

> It is an ecologically balanced system based on minimizing the waste and maximizing the use of all products. The system is economical in water use, simple in technology, and compatible with an uncomplicated division of labor based on household organization. [2]

For the most part, it provided a very modest level of living in return for hard labor to a population bounded by a variety of Malthusian checks and balances. It was a system of production that relied on an abundance of labor and, at least in its latter years, produced a surplus of labor that could find employment only by periodically emigrating to neghbouring countries and beyond. The farming system over this long period of time, either through purposive or natural selection, produced plant and animal varieties well-adapted to each other, the ecosystem and the farm system.

Peasant farmers everywhere, and particularly those in semi-arid areas, are risk adverse. The Yemeni farmer over the ages has been no exception. The integrated agricultural system's primary function was risk aversion to assure minimal food requirements under stress conditions. Production maximization was carried out within this constraint. Vast amounts of the surplus input, labor, were expended to build terraces as a means of preserving and increasing two scarce resources, land and water. Production of drought-tolerant grain and other field crops formed the great bulk of crop production with millet, in particular, performing the function of security against a poor rainfall.

Major reliance for meat and milk production focused on goats, sheep and camels which are most tolerant of drought. The number of cows kept was strictly related to the availability of residue with both crop and animal husbandry organized to complement each other. Oxen, donkeys and camels have been utilized for farm power: ploughing, cultivating, threshing and operating pulley systems for wells. Lastly, the persons responsible for household consumption, women, also had major responsibilities for the production of food.

> In general, women are expected to maintain the house-
> hold physically; men are expected to provide the means
> to do so. This means that women are involved in the
> production and preparation of direct use values (food,
> fuel, feed, and water) and men maintain the working
> capital (land, tools, structures).[3]

The major purpose of the Yemeni agricultural system was to insure against contingencies. Even when the rains were good, it was capable of producing only a very modest surplus over the consumption needs of the farm family.

C. Post Revolution Agriculture

Since 1962 the agricultural system has been subjected to a number of external shocks which appear to have modified the effectiveness of the traditional agricultural production and consumption system. First was the overthrow of the

Imam in 1962, followed by a civil conflict lasting fo

eight years. These were both symbolic and important agent;

of change in the re-entry of Yemen on to the worldwid‹

political and economic scene after centuries of isolation.

On the one hand, a process began which would move Yemeni

agriculture from a self-contained subsistence economy towarc

being a consumer in the international agricultural market

for agricultural products, farm supplies and equipment. On

the other hand, the prolonged and devastating civil war had

a negative effect on all economic activity including

agriculture. Agricultural production and consumption

problems associated with the war were severely exacerbated

with the beginning in 1967 of a seven-year drought. While

statistical evidence for half of the drought period is

unavailable, it is highly likely that over the seven year

period crop production averaged about one-third less than

normal, and in some years output was down as much as

one-half. Livestock numbers also decreased substantially

during this period, and deterioration of the range was

accelerated, although there are no quantitative measures of

the losses. During the latter part of the drought period,

migration began to accelerate with increased demand for

labor by oil-rich neighbors, bringing a third shock to the

Yemeni agricultural system. In 1972-73 recorded remittances

were at a level equal to $124.7 million. By 1976-77

-6-

recorded remittances had exploded to over $1 billion.[4]
The immediate effect on agriculture came in the shift from a
labor surplus agriculture to a fully-employed agriculture
with steadily increasing wage rates resulting from the
rising opportunity cost of labor, rather than from increased
labor productivity. As remittances began to flow back to
Yemen, there were secondary effects on agriculture. Land
prices increased rapidly largely because of a rapid increase
in liquid capital and a highly inelastic supply of land. At
the same time the supply of water, the other scarce
resource, increased somewhat with increased investment,
though water prices at wellheads continued to escalate. On
the consumption side, the inflow of remittances led to a
dramatic rise in food imports and less dependence on
domestically produced foods. However, consumer preferences
caused locally grown crops and livestock to command premium
prices. Between 1972 and 1977 there was a tenfold increase
in food imports, despite an increase in agricultural output
after the end of the drought in 1975. There appears to be
little question "that people are eating better as a
consequence of emigration."[5] However, the 1979 study of
nutrition in Yemen indicates there continue to be nutritional problems, particularly at pre-school age levels.[6]

The changes in the Yemen economy that have occurred
during this period have been profound. The economy has

moved from a largely self-sufficient subsistence agriculture system to an open, service economy. Change and growth within the economy are fueled by the export of labor services, and the major area of growth within the economy is to service the steadily increasing demand mostly for imported consumer goods. While the economy expanded at an annual rate of about 6% per annum during the FFYP period, 1976-77 to 1981, growth in agricultural production is officially estimated to be approximately 1.5 % per annum, substantially less than the probable population growth rate. More significantly, during this period both remittances and private sector imports were twice as large as agricultural production. In this situation, consumption boomed, and in the last year of the FFYP, consumption exceeded GDP by about 7%.[7]

Despite this great burst of consumerism and the growing importance of services, investment in agriculture and related infrastructure increased substantially. This included large investments in secondary road construction, new wells and motorized pumps, trucks for transport of crops to market, agricultural machinery and plant material. It is also true that there was some dis-investment in agriculture where maintenance of capital structures was neglected with the disappearance of cheap and abundant labor.

D. Agriculture During the FFYP

During the FFYP period of 1976/77 to 1980/81 there were
significant changes in agricultural production, but the
amount of growth in agriculture is not clear. Official data
provided by the CPO show that during the five-and-a-half
year period from 1975/76 to the end of 1981 the agricultural
sector grew by only 8.29%, an annual average growth rate of
1.45%, and that the entire growth actually took place during
the last half of 1981. However it is clear that focusing on
growth rates masks changes that took place in the
composition of agricultural output during this period.
There is some reason to believe there was more growth in
crop production than the GDP calculations would indicate,
but there is also reason to believe that animal production,
other than poultry, may have declined. An analysis of
official data shows a significant shift from field grain
crops to high-value, mostly horticultural crops. In 1975/76
the production of field grain crops was 64.6% of total
production by weight, while production of high-value crops
was 33.5%. However, by 1981, field grain crops were only
52.8% of the total while the high value crops increased to
45.9%. As the total quantity by weight of recorded crop
production increased by a modest 5.6% over the period, there
appears to be reason to suggest that the increase in value
added shown in the GDP estimates may be less than that

actually achieved. If one would add to these estimates the increase in _qat_ production over the period, which we estimate to be two to three fold, as well as an increase in _qat_ prices, which have subst.ntially exceeded the inflation rate, this strengthens the case that the value of agricultural production increases has been greater than is generally believed. However, offsetting the above in an unknown amount is a probable decrease in livestock production. All of the team members knowledgeable in any degree about livestock in semi-arid areas are in agreement that the qualititive information indicates that livestock numbers, particularly sheep and goats, declined over the 1976 to 1981 period. The technological reasons for this are set forth in the chapter on Livestock and Poultry and touched on in the chapter on Dryland Crops. In addition, two factors associated with increased income in Yemen over that period tend to support the thesis that livestock numbers have decreased. First, with increased income and construction of schools, more farm children are attending schools. As it is the farm children who usually tend sheep and goats, particularly as they graze the open range, it is probable that this labor shortage has led to a reduction in number of livestock kept by many affected families. Second, with increased ownership of trucks for hauling farm goods and diesel pumps for wells, there has been a substantial decrease in the number of camels, which were traditionally used for long haul transport, and donkeys, which are only of importance today in terrace agriculture.

It does not appear reasonable to draw any definite conclusion about the magnitude of increases in total agricultural output. There has been a definite shift to higher value crops that must have increased income flows to the rural areas. It is not likely that there has been any increase in total livestock numbers. Finally, as the chapter on Livestock and Poultry demonstrates, there has been a strong growth in commercial chicken production.

While the above discussion does little to clarify precise trends in agriculture in Yemen, it does illustrate quite clearly one indisputable fact: much of the analytical work done on agriculture in the Yemen will necessarily consist of asessments based on qualitative information and informed judgments. Given the quality of data, this is the superior method of reaching conclusions about the agricultural sector. Hopefully over the next two to five years the Ministry of Agriculture and Fisheries (MAF) will succeed in its current effort to substantially improve the statistical base.

NOTES

1 Richard F. Nyrop, et.al., <u>Area Handbook for The
   Yemens</u>. Washington, D.C.: U.S. Government Printing
   Office, 1977, p.165.

2 Richard Tutwiler and Sheila Carapico, <u>Yemeni
   Agriculture and Economic Change</u>. Sanaa: American
   Institute for Yemeni Studies, 1981, p. 10.

3 Ibid, p.2.

4 Jon C. Swanson, <u>Emigration and Economic Development:
   The Case of the Yemen Arab Republic</u>. Boulder,
   Colorado Westview Press, 1979.

5 Ibid, p. 65

6 <u>Yemen Arab Republic National Nutrition Survey</u>,
   Washington, D. C., 1979.

7 Of course, GNP exceeded consumption. See Chapter III.

II. THE SOCIAL MILIEU

A. Overview of Yemeni Society

1. Introduction

Yemeni society has undergone a rapid and wide-ranging transformation in the two decades since the Revolution, but it is still necessary to begin with an understanding of traditional social organization. Before 1962 the Zaydi[1] sect of Islam dominated the Central and Northern Highlands, where tribes were influential, and the Shafi'i dominated the Southern Highlands and coastal region, where "feudal" landlords held sway. During the upheaval following the Revolution, regional differences were accentuated and traditional alliances shifted.

In this section only a brief description will be given of the complexities of the social milieu[2]. Identification will be made of significant trends in social and cultural change and the relevance of these trends for assessing the agricultural sector. Specifically, the issues considered will be: social factors inhibiting or limiting agricultural development, factors with potential for promoting expansion of agriculture, and current gaps in the data-base for a socially-responsible agricultural development strategy.

2. Traditional Social Organization.

The area now encompassed by the YAR was not characterized historically by a homogeneous social organization, despite the articulation of a basic threefold hierarchy of Yemeni social structure on the basis of descent:

  (a) Religious Aristocracy (Sada and Quda');

  (b) Tribesmen (rural) and Free Citizens (urban);

  (c) Service Groups, Clients, Pariahs, Slaves, etc.;

In the days of the Zaydi Imamate, the religious aristocracy consisted of Sada (literal descendants of the prophet Muhammad), and learned men and pious scholars of tribal origin. The Zaydi Imams did not replace the tribal system, but simply maneuvered tribal alliances for their own ends.

In the rural Central and Northern Highlands, the tribes dominated the region and formed the bulk of the agricultural labor force. Under tribal customary law, tribesmen had established rights to land and water resources. There was more of an egalitarian emphasis in the north than in the Southern Highlands, which were characterized by less tribal influence and the evolution of a landlord class[3]. The Southern Highlands and coastal region were more susceptible to foreign dominance than the Zaydi areas in the north. A different variety of tribalism evolved in the coastal region, where there was considerable influence from Africa. In the urban areas there was a group of free citizens (merchants, etc.,) who were roughly equivalent in status to the tribal category.

A variety of social groups have existed in Yemen which have not recognized descent status. Some of these were various artisans and service providers asociated with the market. In the rural areas there were client groups who served as barbers, butchers, praise-singers, etc. and were protected under tribal law. In urban areas and some parts of the Southern Highlands were the black Akhdam, who were not equal in status to freed slaves and who did the most menial tasks. Most of the Yemeni Jews lived in cities or in craft-oriented villages. The various market groups and pariahs were under the general protection of tribal law, as were the Sada.

It must be emphasized that social behavior did not necessarily follow the strict hierarchical ordering of the idealized social structure. A number of factors served to modify behavior and these will be considered in the following section on social and cultural change.

3.   Social and Cultural Change

The Republican Revolution in 1962 topped the Zaydi Imamate and appeared to erode the power base of the traditional religious aristocracy. In fact, the Revolution is still in progress and many members of the old power elite have adapted to the changing political climate. In the last two decades North Yemen has not been charcterized by the kind of class struggle that evolved after the British left Aden in the south. Traditional social categories have been redefined and there is a growing sense of national and ethnic unity in the YAR. In this section emphasis will be placed on trends in social change, with a focus on the Yemeni highlands.

a.   Urban vs. rural

The population of the YAR is overwhelmingly rural with an estimated 75% of the population directly engaged in agricultural pursuits. In the days of the Imamate one did not travel in rural areas without a guide from the local tribe. Tribal customary law dominated the rural areas, while formal Islamic law was applied in the urban areas. Although urban/rural bias still exists today, attitudes are changing fast.

As migration for work abroad increased and remittance income was repatriated, there resulted a substantial increase in urban population. The extent of urban sprawl has been particularly evident in the past few years, especially in the city of Sanaa. As more of the rural population takes advantage of the new economic opportunities in the towns and cities (such as shops, taxi service, construction, etc.) two trends can be identified.

(1) Many of the rural areas are exposed to urban and foreign life-styles through the expanding market system and

the media. This has resulted in some rural people emulating
elements of urban life-styles, especially dress and music.

(2) Since many of the new urban populace have recent
roots in the countryside, there is a desire to maintain
links to rural villages. In sum, the rural sector has less
of a self-contained subsistence mentality and the traditional distinction between urban and rural is changing.

b. Economic mobility

The impact of remittances from Yemenis working abroad,
combined with a decline in susbsistence-oriented activities,
has introduced a situation of economic mobility that did not
exist even two decades ago. A butcher can now go to Saudi
Arabia and return wealthier than a Sayyid (descendent of
the prophet) or tribesman. If he returns to his own
village, however, he may still be tainted by his traditional
low status. Thus, many of the low-status service groups
have an incentive to move into the urban areas and become
shop owners, taxi drivers, etc.

Recent ethnographic evidence in Yemen by several
researchers shows that there is a decline in the number of
low-status service providers in the rural sector. Some of
the traditional social customs may soon disappear, unless
tribesmen themselves take up these menial tasks they deigned
before. An exception to this is the singer-musician, who
may command high salaries for performing at weddings.

The process of redefining traditional social roles is a result of the equalizing tendency of the current remittance context. The rich are, in many cases, still rich; but the lot of the traditional poor has also improved enormously. This explains in part why there is little class antagonism as a whole.

c.   Exposure to other cultural life-styles.

Before the 1962 Revolution the Imam kept the gates of his country locked and the minds of his people in isolated ignorance. Yemenis were not only shut off from the outside world, but, to a large degree, tribes were isolated from one another.

Among the most radical introductions of new prosperity is that of the media, with radio and television reaching the most isolated region and poorest hovel. An illiterate population is now exposed to a wide range of films, soap operas, world news, and educational programs. The central government's control of the media has served to bolster its image as well as exposing Yemenis to poetry, music, and dance styles from every part of the country. Television from Aden and Saudi Arabia also reaches many villages. In the past two years, video cassette machines have hit the Yemeni market and video shops have blossomed in the major cities.

The influx of media programs has had a complex effect on the rural populace. News can be transmitted faster and educational programs can reach hundreds of thousands of homes. Although rural Yemenis often comment on violence of American programs and the loose morals of Egyptian soap operas, exposure to new life-styles can serve to strengthen the legitimacy of traditional rural values. Many Yemenis are now more circumspect about the outside world.

d.   Conservatism vs. modernism

In any context of rapid change there is bound to be a conflict between those who see old values eroding away and those who want to adopt new values and life-styles. Some migrants, influenced by experience in Saudi Arabia, desire more segregation of men and women and have more conservative religious ideas. Others are exposed to doctrines of the Muslim Brothers. It is essential for development planners, especially those working with women, to recognize the sensitivities of a growing religious fundamentalism, although most Yemenis have a tolerant attitude towards the strictures of religious observance.

It is useful to make a comparison between religious and political conservatism in Yemen and that found in Iran. In Yemen the rural populace is not being exploited and the central government does not have the power to usurp rights and resources. Thus, there is less fertile ground here for radical-right religious rhetoric, while most Yemenis are oriented towards entrepreneurial and capitalist pursuits.

B. Attitudes Toward Agricultural Activities

1. Valuation of Agricultural Labor

A Yemeni proverb notes that no wealth comes to a man who sits, unless he owns a shop or is a learned man.[4] The fact that Yemenis value hard work is evident in the highland terrace systems, which require intensive labor over the years. It is also clear that farmers who choose a new career often work long hours and live frugally to make their work successful. However, the growing consumption of gat, complemented with alcohol among the rich, is a cause for concern with regard to health and productivity.

Historically, the tribesmen in Yemen valued the cultivation of cereal grains, but disdained cultivation of crops such as vegetables that required immediate marketing.[5] One of the low-class service groups in Yemen was that of the Qashsham, who cultivated the radish, onion, and Chinese chive. The Qashsham often lived in or near a market town and he was not allowed to own land. It was the idea of marketing in a public market, rather than the nature of the crop, that was stigmatized by Yemeni tribesman. It is clear, today, that this traditional tribal disdain for vegetable production has lost most of its sway.[6] A number of tribesmen have become merchants and shop owners. Certain vegetables like tomatoes and potatoes that offer a good return with expanding urban markets are being readily cultivated.

2. Cooperative Ethic

In the rural areas of Yemen there is a long-standing cooperative ethic, which is the basis for the modern LDA movement.[7] Islamic law and tribal customary law emphasize cooperation according to consensus. In traditional tribal society the local shaykh can exercise a right of calling for voluntary aid, such as in the case of repairing a damaged building or field, cleaning a cistern, or building a mosque. In certain agricultural activities there is not only cooperation between family members, but also within the larger community, especially at harvest time.

3. Conservatism vs. Innovation in Agricultural Strategy

Farmers in a subsistence-oriented economy are generally reluctant to switch to new crops and new methods of cultivation. However, over time Yemeni farmers have accepted the introduction of new crops. Coffee only came to Yemen from Ethiopia around the 15th century, but soon became an important export. The Ottoman Turks introduced a number of new crops into Yemen, including maize and tomatoes. Maize is now replacing sorghum on some irrigated land in the highlands. Tomatoes and potatoes have become important crops in the past decade. Farmers are willing to take a risk with a new crop, if it seems to have market potential, as they have sufficient income to buy food in the market. Unfortunately, on much of the rainfed land farmers at present have little option other than the tradiitonal sorghum, barley, and legumes.

C. Social Ramification of Development in the Agricultural Sector

1. Factors Limiting Agricultural Development

a. Fragmentation of land holdings[8]

According to the 1981 Agricultural Census, the average number of parcels per holding ranges from 2.5 in the coastal province of Hode¹Rah to 6.8 in the Central Highland province of Dhamar.[9] It is clear that the fragmentation is more of a problem in the highlands than in the coastal region. There are two fundamental reasons for land fragmentation in Yemen. First, the inheritance system tends to fragmentation of parcels; second, many farmers consider this a way of minimizing risk.

According to Islamic law, a household and its land holdings are to be divided in inheritance according to fixed shares. The daughter, in general, receives half the share of the son, but the situation is more complex than this.[10] There are several traditional mechanisms which help to counteract the problem of fragmentation. Pressure may be exerted on a woman to exchange her right to land for a share in some other form of property, such as a house.[11] This is especially common in areas where water rights are linked to land ownership and there is a desire not to reduce water supply. Also, there is a marrriage preference in the Arab world for the parallel cousin because this keeps land within a genealogical segment over time. There is also a situation of delayed inheritance, where the estate might not be settled until many years after the death of the father. This is beneficial to a woman in that it maintains her link with the natal household for support and political needs and allows her sons to press her claims with her brother(s).[12]

Farmers believe that having several parcels spread out over an area is better than having a large consolidated block of land. This is due to micro-environmental variations in soil fertility, access to water, shade and insolation, etc. Fragmentation is also risk insurance; for example, farmers in wadis often prefer to have some land near the offtake and some farther away. This is because the more valued land near the offtake is also more vulnerable to erosion. Obviously such fragmentation requires mechanisms for cooperation, particularly in irrigated areas.

Fragmentation poses a number of potential production constraints:

(1) Inefficient use of time due to distances required for commuting between fields and transport of fertilizer, produce, etc.

(2) Increased need for labor at peak periods in the agricultural cycle, especially for guarding crops and irri-

gating with spate.[13]

(3) Increased potential for disputes over land boundaries, location of irrigation channels, upkeep of terrace
walls.

(4) Limits switch to well-irrigation.[14]

(5) Limits use of tractors.

The limitations on development imposed by these constraints
may increase over time.

b. Decentralized nature of legal and customary processes

A second factor constraining agricultural development
in Yemen is the decentralized nature of Islamic law and
tribal customary law, particuarly in relation to the allocation of land and water resources. Existing legal and customary processes are designed to serve a subsistence-
oriented economy. Under tribal law it is difficult for a
tribesman's land to be alienated from him. According to
statistics compiled by ECWA, only 5% of the farmers in the
highlands do not own any of the land they farm, while the
figure reaches 35% in the lowlands and coastal region.[15]

In Islamic law the emphasis is on shared access to
water resources, although private ownership is permitted
with specific limitations and obligations. For example,
even though a man may own the land he builds a well on, he
is still obliged to provide water from that well for those
who seek a legitimate purpose, such as drinking or watering

a mount. Furthermore, the prophet Muhammad said that it is wrong to withhold surplus water from another man, for wasting water is a crime against the Islamic community. The sinking of borewells and use of hydraulic pumps generate new and complicated problems in conserving groundwater aquifers and these problems are not fully covered in traditional water law.

In terms of Islamic land and water law, there is no specific code of rules for appropriation and use. Judges apply general principles to differing contexts and often the decisions vary considerably from region to region. Also, most judges interpret Islamic prnciples in the context of local customary practice, a method that the prophet himself followed.[16] Codifying a national land and water law is a logical need, but one that must consider local sensitivities.

c. Migration abroad for non-farmer labor

This report documents the drain of the male labor force and the impact of remittances from Yemenis working abroad in the oil-rich Arab states. Although rates of out-migration differ from region to region, there is clearly a nationwide shortage of male labor for traditional subsistence agriculture. This is evident because of:

(1) abandonment of marginal rainfed terraces in the Central Highlands,[17] and Southern Highlands.[18]

(2)   less intensive upkeep of terrace walls and soils[19] and less attention paid to cleaning irrigation channels.

(3)   increased cost of local farm labor.[20]

(4)   increased role of women in certain agricultural activities, where men once predominated.[21]

One result of the lack of male labor in traditional farming is a change in attitude about the need for hard, low-productive work in rainfed farming. When men who work in Saudi Arabia return, they are not anxious to continue growing sorghum or other subsistence crops. In the valley of al-Ahjur, for example, many men use their training to seek new career opportunities, often outside the valley. Those who continue in agriculture often switch to more lucrative crops like vegetables and qat. Out-migration is stimulating a decline in the traditional, subsistence, agricultural base of the YAR.

d.   Uncoordinated development of rural infrastructure.

In a social system where agriculture is so intimately woven into the ebb and flow of everyday life, expansion of the agricultural sector has direct ramifications on the total development of rural infrastructure. Off-farm income flow has enabled Yemenis to find and develop local infrastructure by self-reliance. Government projects are often several steps behind the rural populace, who often have the capital and contracts to build roads, increase water supply, construct schools, etc. without direct outside or government direction.

Access to new markets through road construction has a powerful impact on cropping strategy. The problem is that farmers may be able to bring in tractors, but there may not be the technical training to effectively utilize the technology or to maintain it. Farmers may obtain new crops, such as citrus, but they lack the know-how to deal with technical aspects of pruning, budding, or controlling pests. Agricultural expansion, in terms of new technology and crops, is in progress, but the long-term effects on the farmers could be disastrous without simultaneous development of the total infrastructure.

e.   Change in market strategy

One of the most dramatic effects of improved transportation networks in rural Yemen is the rapid switch from periodic, dispersed local markets to permanent roadside shops and services. The traditional market served both an economic and a social function, allowing for regional distribution of goods within the area and time for catching up on the latest news and gossip from the traveling merchants. Rural farmers are no longer as dependent on traveling merchants for supplies and marketing of local produce.

Observations in the Central Highlands, Eastern Slopes,

and Southern Highlands clearly indicate that new roadside market settlements continue to open up rapidly. The general pattern is for a gas station to be installed, with its small electricity generator, then the appearance of several tin shacks for selling food items, and consumer goods, as well as restaurants. On the Eastern Slopes such settlements also serve for distributing loads of firewood collected in the waddis.

Another trend in the rural areas is the expansion of major town markets to distribute the expanding flow of imported goods. The market at Shibam in the Central Highlands, for example, has usually been on Friday, although there were also a few permanent shops. Now, however, there is a brisk trade in consumer items and mechanics' services everyday due to the traffic along the main road. While the Friday market still swells, the uniqueness of the occasion has greatly diminished.

There are a number of potential social problems that appear to be resulting from this shift to permanent markets, although this issue requires more detailed analysis.

(1) The generation of waste from cans and paper creates a pollution problem that cannot be met by the traditional attitudes to waste disposal or by the local sanitation facilities (if any exist in a formal sense).

(2) The amount of food garbage and animal bones not

properly disposed of has led to a phenomenal increase of wild dogs in many towns and rural areas. Residents of al-Ahjur complained that a number of people had recently been bitten and became sick.

(3) There is a potential for increased conflict in the market because of traffic jams and the number of people who are from other tribal areas.

(4) Rural farmers have greater access to the market, but many of the social functions of the local market (gossip, talking with important men, etc.) cannot be absorbed in permanent markets and roadside shops.

f.   Ineffective record of previous development projects

One factor limiting the introduction of new development projects is the fact that previous ones have not lived up to expectations of many farmers, who think donor and LDA sponsored projects often fail to benefit them. The media mention the large amounts of money spent on projects, but most farmers think much of this money is wasted or "eaten" by the administrators.

From a farmer's perspective, one of the biggest disappointments is the lack of a viable extension service, despite its existence on paper. IBRD has documented the manifold problems with the existing extension outreach,[22] and Stevenson has noted the high rate of attrition in training extension agents.[23] Regardless of the problems, the rural populace has little reason to think the situation will change soon. Development planners could greatly improve their effectiveness by implementing a visible, yet clearly defined, project and following through to ensure success.

g. The _qat_ habit.[24]

2. Potential for Agricultural Development

Although the constraints are many and complex, there are also social factors which hold potential for expansion of the agricultural sector.

a. Adaptability of indigenous agricultural tradition

An important tradition of rainfed and irrigated agriculture evolved in the southwestern corner of the Arabian peninsula. In the 13th century a number of Rasulid kings in the south planted royal gardens and brought in crops from India and exotic fruits from Syria. A 14th century Yemeni agricultural treatise indicates the wide range of skills at the time and the utilization of earlier Greek and Roman farming skills.[25] Agriculture in Yemen has undergone a series of changes, such as the introduction of coffee in the 15th century. The spread of terraces in the highlands, some of which extend back many centuries, is an indication of the ability of the Yemeni farmer to modify a harsh environment and make it productive.

Unfortunately, the "traditional" agriculture observed in Yemen today is in a state of decline. Terraces are not as intensively worked and effective utilization of slope runoff is rapidly disappearing with a potential for major erosion problems. Without adequate training and access to information, Yemeni farmers still produce best those crops which they have been producing longest.[26] New crops are and should be introduced into the country, but this must be pursued as more than simply a transfer of technology and technique. It is important to consider social ramifications in the economic role of women and potential change in nutrition habits.

b.   Vitality of private sector.

It is evident from the rise of numerous shops and service providers that the private sector in Yemen is active and progressing. Given the capital base, Yemenis are quick to exploit new career opportunities. The rural populace is not sitting back and waiting for the goverment to act; rather, it is attempting to develop roads, power, schools and water supply through local men with the necessary contacts. The LDA movement was created to channel an already vibrant private sector. The cooperative ethic in Yemen extends far beyond the LDA movement, per se. Although farmers are interested in new crops and methods, they lack access to quality farm inputs and information.

Development planners are faced with two options. To continue to work with CYDA and government ministries exclusively may be politically expedient, but the impact on the private sector will be minimal. To provide rural farmers with access to appropriate technology and expert advice in the private sector would have a tremendous impact, but this might conflict with current projects to build up capabilitiy in the ministries. It would appear that development of a strategy in this regard must chart a course through a sensitive issue.

c.   Attraction to rural Yemen

In some countries there is an inevitable process of urbanization that signifies a rejection of the rural lifestyle. In Yemen, however, the rural areas have an idyllic quality in the minds of many Yemenis, even those who are reluctant to live under the rougher conditions. The rural areas are considered cleaner, free of dust, and in many ways healthier than the dusty, crowded cities. To many Yemenis the attraction of rural life is strong. They prefer living and working in rural areas, if modern facilities and amenities could be available. This appreciation of rural life, if joined with employment and income opportunities, would modify rural to urban migration trends.

d.   Developing Yemeni institutions

Many foreign planners make the mistake of assuming that the indigenous professionals are incapable of effectively contributing to development. Yemen has a long literate tradition and in recent years a number of books and articles have been published on the issues in agricultural development.[27] Yet, most donors seem to be unaware of these Arabic sources and fail to utilize some of the recommendations which are relevant to existing cultural sensitivities in the country.

One practical approach that donors can undertake is to strengthen indigenous institutions like Sanaa University both to take advantage of existing Yemeni expertise and build up the institutional capabilities. The development of a faculty of agriculture, for instance, would be a positive step toward coordination of donor policy in the agricultural sector.

e.   Role of media

Another great potential for expanding knowledge of agricultural methods and skills is the use of the media in Yemen. Radio and television have outreach to even the most isolated areas of the country.[28] There is a precedent of farmer-oriented programs on radio,[29] and there is currently a weekly program entitled "Agriculture and the Farmer" on television. The MAF has published (sporadically) papers on various agricultural subjects and there is a regular journal (Ta'awun) which treats the issue of agricultural development.

Myntti has observed that it is not necessary that the

target population be literate to learn subjects directly relevant to work and family life.[30] Even if a person cannot read, he or she invariably knows someone who can read in the rural areas. Bornstein has argued that in many cases it is important to translate a radio program into local dialect.[31] This is especially true for women, who often have a separate dialect, in the coastal region (Tihama). Since almost every Yemeni has access to tape cassettes, there is a potential for this in extension outreach. In the past two years a video cassette craze has swept the country and this offers a promising opportunity for community outreach.

Development programs should emphasize the building up of indigenous quality programming and training of media personnel rather than simply providing educational films. One sensitivity that must be recognized is the delicate nature of the media, politically. In a very real sense, control of the national media represents power. Yet, there is a definite interest in educational programming. One aspect of Yemeni culture that might be utilized is the pervasive role of poetry in describing current events. A poet could be commissioned to provide educational content in a format popular with the rural population.

3.   Gaps in Data-Base Research Needs for Assessing Social Ramifications of Agricultural Development

In-depth and long-term analyses of Yemeni society have only recently been initiated. A number of ethnographic studies have been made in urban and rural areas, but only one major ethnography has yet been published.[32] Access to relevant doctoral dissertations on Yemen is at present limited. There is no available synthesis of recent anthropological study in Yemen.

The following are some of the more pressing social research needs, in order of priority, on the interface between agriculture and Yemeni society:

a. Changes in consumption habits and impact on nutrition

Up to the late 1970s, Yemen's health, education and nutrition indexes were about the lowest in the world. The recent prosperity has obviously ameliorated the situation considerably, but quantitative and qualitative analyses are lacking. The extensive research by Annika Bornstein in the early 1970s needs to be updated. Information should be gathered on changing food preferences and resulting nutrition and health effects.

b. Quantitative analysis of household consumption and budget needs

There is a great deal of conflicting data on the domestic household budget and the decision-making process for distribution of food and other consumption items. While several researchers have extensive experience in rural areas, there has not yet been a focus on the domestic household unit. This is especially important with respect to investment and consumption patterns, nutrition, health, education, division of labor and family planning.

c.   Changing roles of women

Women play a critical role in a subsistence-oriented rural economy. With extensive out-migration of males, changing labor demands, exposure to foreign life-styles and growing affluence, what will happen to traditional female roles and what are future options?

d.   Impact of change in marketing strategy

With the decline of the rural market and growth of permanent roadside markets, there is an inevitable social change. Specifically, how does this shift affect the limited marketing role of women, who did limited marketing of certain goods in local markets? Also, what is the affect of a large number of "strangers" coming into rural areas that used to be strictly segregated? Finally, how does this marketing shift affect time allocation, particularly for agricultural work?

D.   Strategic Considerations

The YAR was almost totally isolated until two decades ago, so it has not undergone a gradual introduction to the West. In the last decade a large amount of development aid has poured into the country, but most of the economic change has resulted from remittances rather than specific donor projects. Yemeni society, not surprisingly, is in a state of rapid and unpredictable change.

In terms of impact on the various segments of Yemeni society, donor agricultural policy should consider the following socio-cultural factors:

1. Yemeni farmers value agricultural labor and are interested in developing the private sector, while government involvement in the rural areas is weak. Donor policy should encourage private initiative by providing access to agricultural inputs, appropriate technology and relevant training. This need not be done exclusively through formal LDA.

2. The role of women in agricultural production may be declining with the switch from subsistence to cash cropping. Given Yemeni cultural sensitivities, donors need to consider non-farm economic roles for women that are not counter to basic cultural norms. Targeting women in specific agricultural projects is not appropriate at this time in the YAR.

3. The lack of adequate information on new farming techniques, on-farm water management and crop protection can be addressed immediately, before a formal extension system is in place, through the creative use of existing media, particularly television and packaged video programs.

4. Donors should avoid attempts to alter directly the problems of land tenure practices, water allocation, expanding qat production and division of labor in agriculture as parts of specific projects; although, all of these are recognized as inhibiting future development. Rather, sensitive issues should be approached through existing Yemeni institutions, such as the MAF or Sanaa University. Promoting social change as part of a specific project is a great risk for donors because project planning rarely includes adequate social soundness assessment and project implementation is usually through expatriate personnel. Donors should ensure that project personnel with continuing links to Yemeni counterparts or population have basic language skills and access to information on cultural sensitivities.

NOTES

1 In fact, the distinction between _Zaydi_ and _Shafi'i_ is not that great in terms of law. The _Zaydi_ polity involved an _Imam_ as spiritual and political leader.

2 For discussion of social organization in Yemen, see Varisco and Adra, "Affluence and the Concept of the Tribe in the Central Highlands of the Yemen Arab Republic," Paper presented at the Amer. Ethnological Soc. Meetings, 1981 (copy in AIYS library), and Tomas Gerholm, _Market, Mosque and Mafraj_, Univ. of Stockholm, 1977 (copy in AIYS library).

3 R. Tutwiler and S. Carapico, _Yemeni Agriculture and Economic Change_, Sanaa: AIYS, 1981, p. 24. It is important to note that _shaykhs_ in the south were not always elected, as were those in the north.

4 Varisco and Adra, _Op. cit._, p. 1.

5 A tribal farmer might grow vegetables for his own use, but he would not market them.

6 Tutwiler and Carapico, _Op. cit._, p. 126.

7 The LDA as an institution will be considered in section IV.

8 See Chapter IV for a discussion of land tenure.

9 YAR, MOA, _Summary of the Final. . ._, June, 1981, p. 24.

10 M. Mundy, "Woman's inheritance of land in highland Yemen," _Arabian Studies_, V., pp. 161-187.

11 C. Myntti, _Women and Development in Yemen Arab Republic_, Eschborn: GTZ, 1979, p. 33.

12 The relationship of a man to his mother's brother (_khal_) is very important in Arab society. For more details, see Najwa Adra, _Qabyala: The Tribal Concept in the Yemeni Highlands_, Ph.D. thesis, Temple University, Philadelphia, Dec., 1982.

13 Tutwiler and Carapico, _Op. cit._, p. 171.

14   A. Bujra, The Politics of Stratification, Oxford, Clarendon Press, 1971, p. 59.

15   ECWA, Crop-Sharing and Land Tenancy Practices in the Yemen Arab Republic, Report No. 1, July 1980, p. 13.

16   Abdullah Maktari, Water Rights and Irrigation Practices in Lahj, Cambridge University Press, 1971.

17   This process of abandonment is documented in: D.M. Varisco, The Adaptive Dynamics of Water Allocation in al-Ahjur, Y.A.R., Ph.D. Thesis, University of Pennsylvania, Dec. 1982.

18   Sr. Alex. Gibb and Partners, Y.A.R., M.O.A. Development of Wadi Bani. Stage I, Preliminary Report, June 1977, p. 2.

19   Swanson, Jon, Draft Report on Beni Awwam, p. 65.

20   Ibid., p. 66

21   C. Myntti, Op. cit., p. 55. Women always had an important role in subsistence agriculture, but the switch to cash cropping results in less of an economic role for women in agriculture.

22   IBRD, Agricultural Sector Study, November 17, 1981, p. 19.

23   Tom Stevenson, Agricultural Extension Services in Yemen: Assessment of Current Programs and Recommendations for Improvement, Sanaa: CID, July 16, 1982, p. 16.

24   See Chapter IV.

25   R.B. Serjeant, "Cereal Cultivation in Medieval Yemen," Arabian Studies, I, pp. 25-181, 1974.

26   Tutwiler and Carapico, Op. cit., p. 178.

27   For an indication of some of this material, see Barbara Croken, Source Materials in Arabic on Rural Development and the Cooperative Movement in the Y.A.R., Cornell University; Working Note #5, October, 1980.

28   See Cornell, Rural Development and Local Organization in Hajja and Hodeidah. Regional Baseline Study Report. Vol. II, 1980, pp. 5ff for details on availability of media in a rural area.

29 See Stevenson, Op. cit., p. 2.

30 C. Myntti, Op. cit., p. 59.

31 Annika Bornstein, Food and Society in the Yemen Arab
    Republic, Rome: FAO, 1974, p. 50.

32 Thomas Gerholm, Op. cit.

III. MACROECONOMICS

A.   Background

The YAR's economy until the overthrow of the Imam in 1962 had been based for centuries almost completely on subsistence agriculture. Since the early and mid 1970s, with the end of the civil war and the boom in demand for foreign workers in Saudi Arabia and the Gulf States, the economy has been undergoing a rapid transformation. Signs of progress are everywhere: paved or upgraded roads connect all major population centers; access roads, generally dirt tracks, connect most villages to this road network; electric power, mainly diesel, and underground water are becoming available even in remote villages; farmers are producing and marketing increasing quantities of higher-value crops; and, imported consumer goods can be found even in the smaller towns and villages.

The principal reason for such change is the increasing inflow of remittances from Yemeni workers in oil-producing countries. From a level estimated in 1970 at about $40 million, some of which came from Yemenis in the U.S., the total inflow rose to over $500 million 1975/76, doubled the next year and peaked in 1977/78 at over $1.4 billion. Since then, officially recorded inflows have declined to just under $1 billion in 1981. In addition, there are remittances of cash and goods sent directly home through private channels that are not recorded by the government. Estimates of this amount vary from one-third to 100% of the official inflow.

These remittances, together with large flows of assistance from neighboring Arab countries, have enabled Yemen to maintain an open economy within a liberal rather than a controlled trade and exchange regime. Recorded imports grew from under $400 million 1975/76 to nearly $1.8 billion in 1981, a level 60% as large as total GDP, even though exports of goods have remained at the very low level of about $10 million annually.

Yemen has thus been transformed from a subsistence economy with a tiny external sector to an open economy propelled by a relatively huge export-oriented service sector. Current prosperity is completely tied to the economic fortunes of its neighbors, particularly Saudi Arabia, and ultimately to the international oil market. Thus, the YAR today is much more dependent on outside economic forces which are volatile. Up to now, the benefits of this situation have been abundantly clear, but some signs of vulnerability are beginning to show: the reduced levels of officially recorded remittances, and the replacement of Yemeni workers by skilled Asian workers in Saudi Arabia and the Gulf, as these countries begin to temper the rate of growth of their economies.

Yemen is still characterized by the UN as a "least-developed" country, despite the profusion of goods in Yemen's shops and the evident rise in national income, production and consumption. Compared to other developing countries, Yemen's domestic production is still at a low level: an estimated $400 per-capita GDP in 1981 at current prices, based on an official population figure of 7.2 million, or an estimated $525 per-capita if a GNP measure is used, one that takes into account the lowest estimated flow of remittances from Yemenis working abroad.[1]

Agricultural production has increased by a little more than 1% annually since 1975/76, a rate substantially less than needed to maintain per-capita food production for Yemen's rapidly increasing population. Thus, the country is increasingly dependent on food imports, while agricultural productivity is low. The shortage of male workers has led to the abandonment of marginal agricultural lands, the neglect of terraces and concomitant spread of erosion in cultivated lands. Industrial output has nearly doubled since 1975/76, but it still accounts for only 8% of domestic production. The population is growing very rapidly, at from just under 3% to over 4.5% annually.[2]

The structure of the economy, including the contrast between gross national savings, estimated at a positive 17% of GNP during the period of the FFYP, and gross domestic savings, which were an estimated negative 20% of GDP during the same period, is discussed in the following section. Also discussed are recent economic trends, the impact of major economic problems on Yemen's agricultural production and the current outlook for Yemen's economy.

B.   Economic Structure and Recent Trends

1.   Production: Domestic and National

Yemen's GDP in current market prices in 1981 totaled just under $3 billion (see table III-1). GDP covers the production of goods and services within Yemen.

When converted into per-capita production, about $400 in Yemen in 1981, GDP gives a picture of the level of economic development relative to other developing countries. In the case of the YAR, as with an increasing number of national economies with a large proportion of workers in foreign countries, GDP magnitudes can be misleading if they are not compared with GNP, a figure which adds to GDP net-factor income. Net factor income is essentially the net total of private transfer receipts paid to the YAR, less private transfer payments paid abroad, and investment income from abroad, less payment to other countries from their investment in Yemen. The most important of these factors for Yemen, as alread noted, is remittances from Yemeni workers in neighboring oil-producing countries. In 1977/78, the peak year for such remittances (see Table III-1), they were 75% as large as total GDP; and even in 1981, they were 35% as large.

GNP is considerably larger than GDP in all recent years (see Table III-1). Moreover, the pattern of expenditures of production is quite different for the two magnitudes. Consumption exceeded GDP by nearly 20% during the FFYP, but as a percentage of GNP, it averaged only 83%. Thus, while gross domestic savings were negative, gross national savings averaged 17%, and financed just over 60% of the nearly 29% of the GNP that was invested (See Table III-2).

2. Sector Origin and Growth of Production

Agriculture, including forestry and fishing, accounts for about 75% of the YAR labor force. It is also the largest single originator of GDP (see Table III-3). Wholesale and retail trade is the second largest sector in all years. However, the importance of both as sources of value-added in the economy is diminishing relative to other sectors. As indicated in Table III-3, agriculture's share of GDP has moved steadily and substantially downward since 1975/76, together with wholesale and retail trade. The value-added shares of construction, manufacturing and transportation have moved up somewhat, and the total of all other sectors, such as defense, education, and health, has increased sharply.

The same pattern emerges from an examination of growth

trends during the FFYP period. While total GDP, in constant
prices of 1975/76, grew by nearly 35% during the FFYP
period, agriculture declined relatively in 1977/78, growing
by a total of only 8%, or just over 1% annually, a rate substantially below that of population growth. Trade also
declined in absolute terms in several of the years shown, so
that its growth over the period was only slightly higher.
Growth in the other sectors, particularly industry and construction but also transportation and communications, was
significantly larger than that for GDP as a whole. As for
trends within the FFYP period, the rate of growth of GDP
peaked in 1977/78, the same year as officially recorded
remittances. With the fall-off of these inflows in subsequent years, the growth of transportation and communications
slowed sharply in 1978//79, while for wholesale and retail
trade it fell in absolute terms. Construction declined
sharply in 1979/80, as money became tighter. Industrial
growth slowed the following year.

3. Investment

Total investment in fixed capital increased during the
FFYP period by an average of 25% annually, the investment in
1981 being 3.4 times as large as in the earlier year (see
Table lIII-5). Figures pertaining to investment in agriculture substantially understate productive investment by farm
families in the rural areas. While official figures show

an investment in agriculture of just 7% of total investment, actual investment was probably at least twice that amount. Investment in infrastructure such as roads is not included nor is much of the investment by farm families in equipment, machinery and physical structures or in infrastructure such as farm-to-market roads.

Housing, as might be expected, accounted for about half of fixed capital investment in earlier years of the period, but its share declined rapidly to a still substantial 28% of the total in 1981 as industry, transportation and communications all increased their share.

Private investment as a share of the total declined from 70% in the earlier years to a very respectable 50% of the total in the later years. The increasing share of public investment, much of it in infrastructure, was made possible mainly by a combination of foreign aid and duties on the rapidly growing volume of imports. Growth of the latter has slowed recently, braking the previously rapid rate of growth in government revenue.

4.   Public Finance

Tax revenues as a percentage of GDP have increased from 10% in 1975/76 to 20% in 1980/81 (Table III-6). Moreover, taxes on income and profits have increased their share of tax revenues from less than 5% in the early years to over 10% starting in 1979/80, a welcome change from the viewpoint

of both equity and the reduction of excessive dependence on
import taxes which were 80% or more of tax revenues until
1979/80.

Government expenditures, however, have more than kept
pace. As percentages of GDP, current expenditures more
than doubled between 1975/76 and 1981, from 12% to 28% of
GDP, while capital expenditures more than quadrupled, from
7% to 29% (Table III-6).3

Thus, the overall budget deficit--before grants and
loans from abroad and government borrowing from Yemen's
banking system--has been growing steadily. While it was
less than $100 million in the years through 1977/78, it
jumped to about $500 million in 1978/79, and by 1981 it had
exceeded $700 million, equal to 25% of GDP.

External financing, which is noninflationary, covered
this deficit through 1977/78; but by 1978/79, despite a very
large inflow of foreign aid, the government was turning
increasingly to the domestic banking system for $110 million
in 1978/79, $400 million the following year, and $340
million (a provisional figure) in 1981 (see Table III-6).

5. Money, Credit and Prices

The impact of expansionary fiscal policies has been
partly offset by the inflow of imports, enabling the growth
of money and credit and the rate of inflation to slow in the
past few years. Annual rates of increase in the Sanaa

retail price index have dropped to about 5-7%, as compared with the 20-25% increases in the mid-seventies. The annual growth of money and quasi-money has fallen from levels of around 50% in the early years of the FFYP period to 10-15% in the latter years. Credit to the private sector has slowed recently, partly because of the reduced rate of growth of private imports concomitant with the slowing in the rate of growth of both GDP and the GNP in Yemen and also because of higher interest rates and more restrained bank lending practices. With Yemen's policy of flexible interest rates and consequent lower rates during the past several months, however, as well as the build-up of excess liquidity in commercial banks, private credit has again expanded.

A large but unquantified variable affecting trade and credit is the volume of goods coming from Saudi Arabia without passing through customs. It seems that a large portion of immigrants' savings is being remitted in the form of goods rather than money, as imported goods in Saudi Arabia tend to be cheaper than in Yemen. These purchases can be brought home with little or no duty paid on them as there is no effective government control of goods crossing the border from Saudi Arabia into Yemen. For example, an imported car which paid minimal duty would be correctly recorded via the car license registration, but in a way which implies it was paid for in Yemen, not as a migrant's remittance from abroad.

6. External Sector

As with the government budget, the balance-of-payments situation implies an increasing capacity for spending and a diminishing inflow of the means to pay for it. Exports of goods, always very small, declined during the FFYP period (see Table III-7), while recorded imports expanded by more than 30% annually, reaching a level in 1981 that was 4.6 times greater than in 1975/76.[4]

Yemen's export of factor services, i.e., workers who remitted to Yemen part of their foreign earnings, increased substantially in the early and mid-seventies, as already noted. In recent years, cash remittances have ebbed, partly because more of the savings are remitted in the form of goods and partly because competition for jobs in Saudi Arabia has increased. Thus, by 1978/79, Yemen's current-account balance changed from a positive $300 million the preceding year to a negative $330 million. While the inflow of foreign aid and other capital enabled YARG to add to its foreign-exchange reserves in that year (1978/79), it drew from them in all subsequent years, especially in 1980/81.

Reserves (net foreign assets) of the Central Bank consequently fell from over $1.5 billion on June 30, 1979 to under $1 billion by the end of 1981 and to under $800 million by June 30, 1982. Total foreign debt had increased to $2,125 milllion by June 30, 1982, of which $1,150 million was disbursed.[5] Debt service, although rising, has remained low compared with other developing countries, only $59 million in 1981, owing to the government's ability to obtain large amounts of concessional aid.

Yemen's exchange rate is pegged to the U.S. dollar (YR 4.5 to $1) and is in effect under-pinned by the Saudi Riyal. The Yemeni Riyal has thus appreciated significantly vis-à-vis many other currencies as the U.S. dollar and the Saudi Riyal have strengthened.

C.   Major Economic Problems

Budget deficits are an immediate problem facing the YARG, with clear ramifications for agriculture. Although their inflationary impact has been largely offset up to now by Yemen's ability to increase imports, financed by workers' remittances and foreign aid, such offsets are probably less likely to be as large in the future. Thus, the YARG is faced with the choice of: (1) continued deficits, with the attendant inflationary pressure, high demand for imports and consequent exacerbation of balance-of-payment deficits; (2) reduced public investment and services for agriculture and other sectors; and/or, (3) increased taxes.

The second major economic problem facing Yemen at this time is the very large deficit in the YARG's current-account balance during the past few years, even after the offsetting entry of private transfer receipts from Yemeni workers abroad. Expansion of Yemen's exports and foreign aid is the obvious recourse, but this is essentially a long-term solution. Stepping up or maintaining worker-remittance inflows is a solution which could yield intermediate and even short-term benefits. Without some such action, agriculture and other economic sectors in Yemen could face a situation of shortages in investment goods of all types, as well as of imported foods that are now essential in Yemeni consumption patterns.

The importance of the problem, both overall and for agriculture, as well as the opportunities associated with the problem, suggest the advisability of a special study investigating possible means to increase the inflow of remittances.

D. Workers' Remittances

Increasing the inflow of workers' remittances requires, first of all, more information of the characteristics of Yemeni workers' skills, earnings, savings and motivations. There appears to have been no systematic attempt to organize and quantify information on factors such as the numbers of persons working, by approximately duration of stay, ages, marital status, pre-departure skills, skills acquired abroad, opportunities for acquiring and utilizing new skills, wage rates, savings per worker, location of non-transient savings, and proportions remitted by various channels. Moreover, no one in Yemen seems to be aware of Saudi Arabia's current and prospective needs and preferences for foreign workers; nor is it known what measures might encourage Yemeni workers to save and remit more of their earnings.

The lack of accurate information on the number of Yemeni workers abroad is evident as one talks to officials and other knowledgeable observers, both Yemeni and foreign. Officially, the number of migrants was placed at 1.2 million in 1975 and nearly 1.4 million in 1981,[6] while most observers suspect the current number is about 400,000. Since migrants are overwhelmingly males and given that the 1975 census figure show an excess of 250,000 females over males in both the 10 to 59 and 15 to 54 age groups, then the 400,000 estimate for migrants seems more reasonable.[7] Similarly, per-capita annual remittances of about 2,500 based on 400,000 migrants, seem more reasonable than estimates of $800 based on 1.2 million migrants, given the estimated annual earnings of $7,500 in Saudi Arabia and the known savings propensities of Yemeni workers.

If accurate information were available on these and other questions, it might be feasible to adopt measures to increase placement of Yemenis in higher paid jobs abroad than would otherwise be possible. Pre-departure training in the skills required for jobs where Yemenis would have a comparative advantage vis-à-vis non-Arab-speaking Asians might turn out not to be too costly or difficult. Or arangements might be made for some training in the employing country; this is being done, but on individual initiative, not systematically through government or private agreements. Organized recruitment of migrants for particular openings might also be feasible. This is a very common service offered by Asian contractors and could raise substantially the average earnings of Yemeni workers.

2.   More Productive Uses of Returning Workers

Yemen is changing from a low-cost, labor-surplus economy to a relatively high-cost, labor-short economy. It is therefore all the more important that returning workers utilize any newly acquired skills to increase overall labor productivity in Yemen. Again, systematic information is needed to enable the YARG to devise appropriate measures-- perhaps informational only, but certainly not regulatory--to encourage such productive use. Some returning migrants, for example, with newly acquired mechanical skills might require some capital or credit assistance to set up shop to fully use their skills for local benefit.

3.   More Productive Use of Remittances

Locating investment opportunites for private capital in Yemens' agriculture, industry, and other sectors beyond those which are apparent to returning migrants or their

families might well be more difficult than maintaining/-
increasing remittances or using returning migrants more pro-
ductively. Guaranteeing high-investment bonds for capital-
short private ventures might be worthwhile, as already noted
above, but it is not a measure to be undertaken lightly.
Finally, while public-sector investments in high-priority
infrastructure have contributed substantially to economic
growth in Yemen, it is by no means clear that the YARG could
or should try to mobilize remittances for such additional
activities, especially since it is mostly local resources
that are needed.

F.   The Economic Outlook

1.   The SFYP

Annual growth rates for the SFYP period (1982-86) are
projected at 7% for GDP, 4.2% for agricultural production,
14.5% for manufacturing and 12% for mining. These compare
with realized annual rates of growth during the FFYP of
nearly 6% for GDP, about 1% for agriculture, nearly 12% for
manufacturing and 18% for mining.

The uses of GDP and GNP are scheduled to differ substantially between the two plan periods. Consumption is to grow
at 5% annually from 1982 to 1986, which is less than the
growth projected for GDP. Consequently, consumption is to
be just under 110% of GDP in 1986, instead of the current
rate of more than 120%. If these targets were realized,

domestic savings would become substantially less negative. National savings, including workers' remittances, would finance nearly half of total investment (49.2%). Net loan disbursements are projected to finance most of the remainder (46.2%) and direct net foreign investment finances the balance (4.6%).

Investment is to increase by about 1% annually, compared with the nearly 25% annual growth during the FFYP period. By 1986, it is to account for about 34% of GDP, compared with the current 45%. Imports are also to increase by only 1%, so that their relationship to gross domestic product would be significantly smaller in 1986, just over 55% compared with about 75% in 1981. The rationale for projecting annual growth rate of 7% for GDP, while increasing imports and investments only 1% per year, is not clear.

Agriculture's share of fixed investment is scheduled to double from the FFYP levels of around 7%, to a projected 15.8% of the total. The share of manufacturing and mining is projected at 15.7%, with an additional 8.3% planned for utilities, almost all in the public sector. Transportation and communications and government services, are scheduled to receive 16.5%. The public and mixed private-public sectors are to absorb two-thirds of fixed capital investment, apart from the government-services sector, mostly in transportation and communications (14%), agriculture (11%), manufacturing (8.6%) and utilities (8.1%) of the total). Strictly private-sector investmewnt is to be mainly in housing (12.4%), trade (7.1%), agriculture (4.8%) and manufacturing (3.9% of the total).

Imports are scheduled to increase by only 1% annually, while workers' remittances are projected at an annual level of about $1 billion, compared with an annual, average, recorded level of $1.2 billion during the FFYP, a high of $1.4 billion in 1977/78, and a low of just under $1 billion in 1981. Together with a projected annual 14.3% expansion of exports, these trends would lead to a gradual reduction of the current-account deficit by 1986 to a level of under $600 million in 1981 prices.

Capital inflows by 1986 are projected at $600 million for drawings on loans, plus an additional $35 million in grants. Of this $635 million, the Plan categorizes nearly $300 million as foreign aid. The Plan also foresees over $75 million in direct foreign private investments in Yemen. These inflows would lead to a start on replenishing foreign-exchange reserves by 1985, so that reserves for the entire Plan period would end up about the same as in 1982, if the Plan's projections were realized.

The Plan also foresees a gradual rise in domestic revenues, including non-tax revenues, from the 20-25% of GDP levels during most of the FFYP period to proportions exceeding 30% by 1985. These revenues are rather optimistically projected to exceed current expenditures. This might or might not be sufficient to pay for the government's share of the $4.1 billion in government or mixed government/private investments projected for the SFYP period. It would seem, however, that some deficit in the overall budget could be expected if all investments and other aspects of the plan were realized, which would mean some recourse to financing by the Central Bank and commercial banking system.

2. Overall Assessment

a. Public finance.

Reducing the budget deficit to more manageable proportions will not be easy. The need for the government to provide basic services in both rural and urban areas, for military purposes and for socio-economic reasons, precludes drastic reductions in expenditures. The YARG has planned in the SFYP to finance or facilitate large-scale investments in utilities and transportation as well as in agriculture and industry.

On the revenue side, the YARG has successfully increased tax revenues during the FFYP period. Moreover, some of the additional measures to mobilize domestic resources through noninflationary means, which have been recommended by international organizations, are likely to be adopted by the YARG. However, while the combination of all the recommended measures might be adequate under favorable circumstances, none by itself is likely to come anywhere near meeting YARG's financial needs. Substantial increases in tax revenues from foreign trade are not likely, since higher rates would encourage smuggling. A rapidly increasing volume of taxable imports is also unlikely in view of the fall-off in worker remittances to pay for them. Substantial increases such as a tax on irrigated or qat land in the near future seem possible, and government should pursue this avenue. In the immediate term, though, government is inclined to take the easy route of increased borrowing from the domestic banking system, which would strengthen inflationary pressures. Government might continue to seek as much foreign aid as possible from neighboring countries, a relatively painless economic option, but a risky prospect now in view of other problems.

On balance, therefore, substantial budget deficits in the SFYP period seem more likely than the budget surpluses projected in the second half of the SFYP. The extent of inflationary pressures and their impact on prices, money and credit, and the balance of payments remain to be seen.

b.   Production and investment.

The YAR has relied largely on market forces in an open economy to stimulate and guide private-sector efforts during the FFYP period, with the government supporting these efforts by extensive infrastructure improvements. During this period, there has been large-scale assistance by citizens working abroad and from neighboring Arab states. The results have been impressive, but maintaining this progress, or speeding up its rate, as the SFYP projects, may well depend on whether these flows can be sustained during the SFYP period. It will also be influenced by whether the YARG will have the resources to finance the very large volume of government and mixed government/private investment planned.

The government is encouraging private foreign and domestic investment by allowing tariff exemptions on imported investment goods and some materials, income-tax holidays and complete freedom for profit repatriation. However, it is emphasizing import substitution in its project-selection criteria, which is a high-cost, low-return strategy for Yemen, given the country's dearth of revenues, high labor costs, low labor productivity, and access to cheap, high quality goods easily available in Saudi Arabia. The YAR has substantial opportunites for increasing its agricultural production, particularly of fruits and vegetables. Some of this increased production can be marketed in Saudi Arabia, provided international marketing standards are met.

c.   Balance of Payments.

Both opportunities and problems abound in the areas of

foreign-exchange earnings and savings. Regarding imports, it will clearly be difficult for the government to restrain import growth to the 1% annual increase targeted in the SFYP at the same time that it increases the share of investment goods in the total.

Increased exports cannot make a major contribution to resolving Yemen's near-term balance-of-payments problems, but foreign-exchange earnings from this source could be substantially increased. Much more important now, however, is the initiation of government action to encourage greater inflow of remittances. For if Yemen is to extricate itself from the current position of rapidly drawing down its foreign exchange reserves, which may now be approaching the $500 million level and be only sufficient for 3 to 4 months' imports, workers' remittances offer the only major opportunity apart from increased foreign aid.[8]

TABLE III-1
GDP and GNP

(in current market prices, YR millions)

	1975/76	1976/77	1977/78	1978/79	1979/80	1980/81	1981 YR mil	1981 $ mil
1. GDP	4,935	6,487	8,220	10,166	11,919	12,630	12,949	2,878
2. Net Factor Income	2,239	4,014	5,262	4,276	5,680	4,591	4,000	889
a. Private transfer receipts	2,363	4,561	6,351	5,595	6,118	4,936	4,444	988
b. Private transfer payments	-306	-770	-1,446	-1,845	-1,175	-888	-897	-199
c. Net investment income	182	223	357	526	737	543	453	101
3. GNP	7,174	10,501	13,482	14,442	17,599	17,221	16,949	3,766
4. GDP/GNP (%)	69	62	61	70	68	73	76	.
5. GNP/GDP (%)	145	162	164	142	148	136	131	131

Notes to Table:

Source of data: CPO, Statistical Year Book, 1981. P. 321 for row 1; p. 184 for rows 2a and 2b; p. 340 for row 2c; other rows derived.

Conversion rate for 1981 dollar column: YR 4.5 = $1.

Minor discrepancies are due to rounding.

63

TABLE III-2

GDP and GNP Expenditures

(in current market prices, YR millions)

	1975/76	1976/77	1977/78	1978/79	1979/80	1980/81	1981 YR mil	1981 $ mil	1976/77 to 1981 $ mil
1. CONSUMPTION	5,583	8,323	8,894	11,991	14,344	15,351	15,677	3,484	
a. Private	4,902	7,462	7,652	10,205	12,154	12,812	12,707	2,824	
b. Government	681	861	1,242	1,786	2,190	2,539	2,970	660	
2. GROSS INVESTMENT	1,004	1,391	3,567	4,475	5,237	5,520	5,778	1,284	25,968
a. Fixed Capital	849	1,496	3,160	4,445	4,882	5,413	5,600	1,244	
b. Stock Changes	155	-105	407	30	355	107	178	40	
3. NET EXPORTS OF GOODS AND NONFACTOR SERVICES	-1,652	-3,227	-4,241	-6,300	-7,662	-8,241	-8,506	-1,890	
a. Exports	214	279	242	474	803	805	1,130	251	
b. Imports	-1,866	-3,506	-4,483	-6,774	-8,465	-9,046	-9,636	-2,141	
4. GDP AT MARKET PRICES	4,935	6,487	8,220	10,166	11,919	12,630	12,949	2,878	62,371
5. Net Factor Income	2,239	4,014	5,262	4,276	5,680	4,591	4,000	889	
6. GNP AT MARKET PRICES	7,174	10,501	13,482	14,442	17,599	17,221	16,949	3,766	90,194
MEMO ITEMS									
7. Gross Domestic Savings	-648	-1,836	-674	-1,825	-2,425	-2,721	-2,728	-606	-12,209
8. Gross National Savings	1,591	2,178	4,588	2,451	3,255	1,870	1,272	282	15,614
9. Consumption/DGP (%)	113	128	108	118	120	122	121	120	120
10. Savings/DGP (%)	-13	-28	-8	-18	-20	-22	-21	-20	-20
11. Investment (%)	20	21	43	44	44	44	45	42	42
12. Consumption/GNP (%)	78	79	66	83	82	89	92	92	83
13. Savings/GNP (%)	22	21	34	17	18	11	8	8	17
14. Investment/GNP (%)	14	13	26	31	30	32	34	34	29

Notes: CPO, op. cit., p. 333 for rows 1-4, Table III-1 for row 5; other rows derived.

TABLE III-3
GDP by Sector of Origin
(in percentages of total)

	1975/76	1976/77	1977/78	1978/79	1979/80	1980/81	1981
1. Agriculture, fishing, forestry	43	40	33	32	31	30	30
2. Manufacturing, mining, utilities	7	5	7	7	8	8	8
3. Construction	6	8	11	11	9	9	9
4. Transportation and Communications	3	4	4	4	4	4	4
5. Trade	20	20	20	18	19	18	17
6. Other (residual)	21	23	25	28	29	31	32
7. GDP	100	100	100	100	100	100	100

Notes: The percentages are derived from data on GDP at market prices, given in current rials on CPO, p. 321. The total has been adjusted to remove import duties and add back in "imputed bank service charges." Thus, the total is similar in concept to GDP at factor costs, data on which are given on p. 313. The two series differ in magnitudes, partly because of the "bank service charges." Percentage orders of magnitude do not differ.

65

TABLE III-4

RATES OF GDP GROWTH BY SECTOR

(in percent)

	1975/76	1976/77	1977/78	1978/79	1979/80	1980/81	1981	1976/77 to 1981
1. Agriculture, fishing, forestry	3.0	-8.0	-10.6	16.5	4.3	5.1	3.1	8
2. Manufacturing, mining, utilities	11.3	8.8	18.6	17.2	14.7	6.4	2.8	90
3. Construction	53.8	31.8	37.0	13.7	-17.4	-2.3	2.6	70
4. Transportation and communications	3.4	6.7	25.0	4.0	1.4	2.8	1.4	47
5. Trade	20.6	-0.4	4.6	-2.4	10.4	-0.4	-2.5	9
6. GDP	11.0	5.1	8.3	6.6	5.5	3.8	1.2	34
7. GDP (YR millions, constant prices)	4,935	5,186	5,615	5,988	6,318	6,555	6,635	

Notes

All data are from CPO, p. 307 and are given in constant prices of 1975/76.

Data for 1974/75 (not shown), which were used to derive the total and annual average growth rates shown

TABLE III-5

INVESTMENT

	1975/76	1976/77	1977/78	1978/79	1979/80	1980/81	1981
Fixed Capital Formation (YR mil., constant prices)	849	1,224	2,190	2,667	2,681	2,796	2,854
By Economic Sector (%)							
Agriculture, fishing, forestry	7	4	7	7	6	7	8
Manufacturing, Mining, utilities	6	16	13	14	15	19	21
Construction	1	3	5	5	6	6	6
Transportation and Communications	26	17	26	23	31	28	24
Housing	49	50	34	30	28	27	28
Other sectors	11	10	15	21	14	13	13
Total fixed capital	100	100	100	100	100	100	100
By type of owner							
Private	70	69	51	50	54	50	49
Public	30	31	49	50	46	50	51
Stock Changes (YR mil.)	155	-77	282	28	191	55	91
Gross Investment (YR mil.)	1,004	1,147	2,472	2,695	2,872	2,851	2,945

Notes:
Absolute data, shown in YR millions, are in 1975-76 prices. Fixed capital and gross investment data are from CPO, p. 346 and p. 343 respectively; stock changes were derived from p. 343 and 346.

Sector allocation percentages were derived from current price data on p. 348; ownership percentages, also in current prices, are from p. 347.

67

TABLE III-6

SUMMARY OF GOVERNMENT FINANCES

(YR million)

	1975/76	1976/77	1977/76	1978/79	1979/80	1980/81	1981 YR mil	1981 $ mil	Project 1982
1. Domestic Revenues	604	1,284	1,954	2,147	2,674	3,132	4,204	934	3,850
a. Tax Revenues	492	1,077	1,583	1,732	2,079	2,786	3,078	684	
(1) Import Duties	394	929	1,305	1,386	1,610	2,037	2,248	500	
(2) Income & Profit Taxes	23	40	101	139	211	296	347	77	
(3) Other	75	108	177	207	258	453	483	107	
b. NonTax Revenues	112	207	371	415	595	347	1,126	250	
2. Current Expenditures	616	841	1,249	1,847	2,427	3,367	3,627	806	4,100
a. Defense	304	430	545	794	1,018	1,332	1,333	296	
b. Health and Education	74	93	200	365	496	718	847	188	
c. Other	238	318	504	688	913	1,317	1,447	322	
3. Balance on Current Operations	-11	443	705	300	247	-235	577	128	-250
4. Capital Expenditures	361	603	1,166	2,618	2,492	n.a.	3,807	846	4,450
a. Development	293	404	780						
b. Capital Transfers	39	141	276						
c. Defense	29	58	110						
5. Overall Deficit	-373	50	-462	-2,318	-2,245	n.a.	-3,230	-718	-4,700
6. External Financing	657	606	750	1,818	976	1,470	2,377	528	2,700
a. Commodity & Project Loans	213	188	330	495	559	740	950	211.	1,200
b. Cash Loans	—	19	37	16	—	408	228	51.	
Less Repayments	-14	-19	-26	-44	-34	-287	-265	-59.	
c. Cash Grants	458	418	409	1,351	451	609	1,464	325	1,500
7. Domestic Financing (Net)	-257	-532	-51	495	1,792		1,534	341	2,000
Change in deposits	-269	-485	-50						
a. Central Bank	12	-47	-1						
b. Commercial Banks	-27	86							
8. Statistical Adjustment		-237		5	-523		-681	-151	—
Tax Revenues as a % of GDP	10.0	16.6	19.3	17.0	17.4	22.1	23.8	n a	n a
Deficit as a % of GDP	7.6	2.3	5.3	22.8	18.8	n.a.	24.9	n a	n a

Notes to Table III-6

1. Sources

   a. Domestic revenues and current expenditures are from CPO, pp. 186-190; they are consistent with earlier data used by the IMF and World Bank.

   b. Capital expenditure statistics for 1975/76 to 1977/78 are from World Bank reports; for 1978/79 to 1982 (projected), from IMF reports.

   c. External financing data from CPO, p. 184; they are consistent with earlier statistics used by the IMF and World Bank.

   d. Domestic financing data for 1975/76 to 1977/78 are from World Bank reports; 1978/79 to 1982 projected, they were derived as a residual.

   e. Figures on current operations and the overall deficit were derived in all years.

   f. The statistical adjustment figures were derived for 1975/76 to 1977/78; they are from IMF reports for 1978/79, 1979/80 and 1981.

   g. Tax revenues and the overall deficit as percentages of GDP were derived.

2. Coverage

   a. Domestic revenues exclude grants for budgetary support; these grants are included under external financing.

   b. Current expenditures exclude loan repayments.

   c. Increases in deposits, under domestic financing, are shown as negative entries; i.e., preceded by a minus sign.

   d. The statistical adjustment, according to World Bank reports, reflects lags in recording, exchange-rate-valuation adjustments associated with external financing, and other errors and omissions.

TABLE III-7

BALANCE OF PAYMENTS

(YR millions)

	1975/76	1976/77	1977/78	1978/79	1979/80	1980/81	1981 YR mil	1981 $ mil
1. Trade Balance	-1,666	-3,200	-4,103	5,613	-6,926	-7,580	-7,821	-1,738
a. Exports f.o.b.	55	84	32	13	32	72	47	10
b. Imports c.i.f.	-1,721	-3,284	-5,626	-5,626	-6,958	-7,652	-7,868	-1,748
(Government)	(-269)	(-292)	(-605)	(-1,207)	(-1,387)	(-1,261)	(-1,638)	(-364)
(Private)	(-1,452)	(-2,992)	(-3,529)	(-4,419)	(-5,571)	(-6,391)	(-6,230)	(-1,384)
2. Non-Factor Services, Net	196	197	219	-161	-2	-118	-232	-52
3. Factor Services, Net	2,239	4,014	5,262	4,276	5,680	4,591	4,000	889
a. Workers' Remittances, Net	2,057	3,791	4,905	3,750	4,943	4,048	3,547	788
b. Investment Income, Net	182	223	357	526	737	543	453	101
4. Current Account Balance	769	1,011	1,378	-1,498	-1,248	-3,107	-4,052	-900
5. M&LT Capital, Net	712	659	792	1,939	1,213	1,952	2,764	614
a. Official Grants	513	470	452	1,403	503	668	1,516	337
b. Official Loans, Net	199	188	340	536	710	1,284	1,248	277
(Disbursements)	(213)	(207)	(366)	(566)	(743)	(1,324)	(1,293)	(287)
(Repayments)	(-14)	(-19)	(-26)	(-30)	(-33)	(-40)	(-45)	(-10)
6. Other Capital, Net	-60	-171	-157	323	26	-842	-211	-47
7. Change in Reserves (Increase = -)	-1,421	-1,499	-2,013	-764	9	1,997	1,494	333
a. Central Bank	-1,245	-1,990	-1,733	-912	546	2,073	1,494	332
b. Commercial Banks	-177	491	-280	-148	-537	77	5	1

Notes:

Source:
CPO, pp. 184 and 340, except that "other capital" was derived as a residual, and repayments of official loans after 1977/78 were estimated. Part 6 includes errors, omissions and valuation adjustments.

NOTES

1 The World Bank rates YAR as a middle-income economy.
   With an estimated 1980 GNP per capita of $430, it is in
   the same league as Indonesia, Mauritania and Senegal,
   just below Angola and Liberia. Even a cursory
   association with these countries draws an immediate
   response that average consumption and investment in
   rural Yemen are far above those in any of these other
   five countries.

2 CPO, YAR, Statistical Year Book 1981, pp. 33 and
   342.

3 Total government expenditure accounted for 57% of GDP,
   and 54.5% of GNP in 1981. Observation would indicate
   that the public sector does not dominate the economy to
   the extent purported by the statistics and that both
   GDP and GNP are probably under-reported.

4 The largest volumes of imports come from Saudi Arabia
   ($363 million of recorded imports in 1980), Japan
   $239 million), France $148 million), and West Germany
   ($110 million). The U.K., Italy, China, and the
   Netherlands have $90 to $100 million; then Singapore
   ($73 million), South Korea ($55 million), the U.S. ($53
   million), and India ($52 million). The diversity of
   import sources is apparent in almost any store visited.

5 Central Bank of Yemen, Financial Statistical
   Bulletin, April-June 1982, pp. 7 and 28.

6 CPO, Op. cit., p. 33.

7 The totals for males and females aged 10-59 are 1.19
   and 1.42 million, respectively, while they are .87 and
   1.14 million for the 15-54 group.

8 Data on private transfer receipts for the first half
   of 1982 were released by the Central Bank during the
   last few days of the team's stay in Yemen. These
   totaled $582 million--or $1,164 million for the entire
   year, if the levels were to be maintained. This
   increase of $177 million in recorded transfers for 1982
   would be most welcome, if it materialized. Note,
   however, that on the same assumption, private transfer
   payments would be $82 million higher, yielding a net
   increase of just under $109 million.

IV. AGRICULTURAL INSTITUTIONS

A. Women's Role in Agriculture

The role of a woman in agriculture derives from her place in the social structure as determined by customary rules, norms and Islamic law. From the agricultural production, marketing and consumption perspective, the following customs and laws are most important.

1. When a woman marries, her rights are transferred from the father to the husband. Most importantly, this means that the husband acquires tne rights to the woman's labor.

2. Women inherit property;

> ...as a daughter: half the share of her brother (as an only child: half the total inheritance). As a mother: 1/6 of the total inheritance. As a wife 1/8 of the total inheritance".[1]

As women may inherit land, this increases fragmentation of agricultural holdings. This tendency towards land fragmentation is often countered in the patrilineal, patriarchal Arab society of Yemen through parallel cousin marriage.

3. Woman's wealth, irrespective of whether it is obtained through bridewealth, inheritance or, much more rarely, earned income, is hers to spend or save as she chooses. It is not used to support the household, which is the responsibility of the husband. A woman's bridewealth,

inheritance or other assets are, however, managed by a male member of the family.

4.   Women generally do not engage in commercial activities; most buying and selling is done by men. While women do numerous tasks in subsistence production, they do much less or none at all if agricultural production becomes commercialized.[2]

> Female work predominates in poor areas with the cultivation of subsistence crops such as sorghum. In wealthier areas, where traditional and modern cash crops are cultivated, women play a less important role even if sorghum is also cultivated. If anything, 'development' brings differentiation in wealth, and those with greater wealth can afford the prestige of secluding their women and hiring daily labor.[3]

Within this framework the division of labor between the sexes is clearly demarcated.

> In general, women are expected to maintain the household physically; men are expected to provide the means to do so. This means that women are involved in the production and preparation of direct use values (food, fuel, feed and water) and men maintain the working capital (land, tools, structures).[4]

Women's work is again allocated within the typical Yemeni's extended household on the basis of seniority. Decisions on what is done and who does it are made by the wife of the head of the household. Older women do light work such as feeding and milking cows by hand. Younger women do the heavy work both in the house and in the field. Young girls help cook, fetch water, take care of small livestock and work in the fields.

> In sum, women have a considerable influence on the household whether it be extended or nuclear. Their power is restricted in that they do not participate in the public world of the market, nor have ultimate control over the monthly household expenditures. All final decisions rest with the males who are responsible for the support of the household.[5]

In addition to doing all of the work associated with running the household--collecting fuel, fetching water, washing clothes, cooking, baking, grinding grain, etc.--women perform a wide variety of tasks in subsistence agriculture. Women's agricultural tasks are performed year around, while the work of men as it relates to crop production activities is more apt to be seasonal. However, the extent of women's involvement in agricultural labor is inversely related to wealth and social status, as well as the commercialization of agriculture. While the wife of the ordinary farmer may labor almost every day in the fields, the wife of a wealthy landowner may not work at all in the fields and take up the veil. The general pattern of the division of labor in crop production for the ordinary farmer is as follows:[6]

Terrace construction:	Men
Leveling land	Men
Hard tilling	Men
Ploughing	Men, boys from about age 12
Planting grains	Women and men
Planting coffee/qat	Men
Applying manure	Women and men
Applying chemical fertilizer	Men
Weeding	Women and men

Applying insecticides	Men
Irrigation	Men
Bird scaring	Children, old women
Stripping sorghum leaves	Women, or family
Harvesting grains	Women and men
Harvesting coffee/qat	Men
Cutting alfalfa	Generally women
Picking grapes	Men
Picking vegetables	Men
Threshing	Women and men
Winnowing at harvest	Women and children
Winnowing small amounts of grain	Women

When males migrate for short-term or long-term work abroad, efforts are made to provide access to male labor for wives and families left behind. A woman does not simply take over male activities. It is common for a man to make arrangements with a relative or neighbor to continue agricultural activities. The re-allocation of time on the farm, where males have left for work abroad, is parallel to the pattern of remittance transfer. A man does not send money directly to the females of the household; rather, he sends to a male relative or remittance agent, who acts on behalf of the wife.

Women have a dominant role in subsistence agriculture, but sometimes women will work for pay at traditional agricultural tasks. In the Central Highland valley of al-Ahjur, for example, young girls will often be hired within a local area for stripping sorghum leaves or harvesting. In al-Ahjur both women and men received the same pay (YR 60 or $14) for a day's work in 1982. In 1979, in the Southern Highlands, however, Myntti reported that women received only half of what men earned for carrying water, small stones and mud at construction sites.[7] The only other public employment roles traditionally open to women in rural Yemen have been specific to social status. Thus, there are female singers, female healers, and low-status women who performed menial tasks. In general, however, it was not considered appropriate for rural women to work in public for wages. In recent years new roles have opened, such as school teachers, nurses, bank clerks, secretaries, etc., but most of these are not in rural areas.

The evidence indicates that, at least in the short or medium term, the decline in importance of subsistence agriculture and the increasing importance of commercial agriculture reduces the relative participation of women in agricultural activities. Since other job opprtunities are limited, the number of women actively engaged in the labor force may well decline. At the same time, job opportunities for unskilled males in Saudi Arabia seem to be declining. Because hired male labor or capital in Yemen will be substituted for female labor with increased commercialization of agriculture, the movement of women out of the labor force may have an adverse effect on net farm family income. This should not adversely affect the absolute private wealth of women, although it will clearly decrease female participation in the farm economy.

B.   Land Tenure

The land tenure situation is complicated and not adequately understood. The current pattern of land distribution, ownership and use has largely been determined by the close interrelationship of land and water rights. Islamic inheritance laws, endogamous marriage patterns, the relative scarcity of available land in relation to both total land area and population and, in recent years, emigration and remittances. There are also geographical differences in tenure patterns between the highlands and the coastal lowlands.

Since so little is known about land tenure on the Eastern Slopes, this area is excluded from the following discussion.

The most notable features of land ownership and operation in Yemen are the size of holding and amount of land fragmentation. Based on an agricultural census of governorates covering both lowland and highland areas, two-thirds of the farms were less than one ha., nearly one-quarter were less than a fourth of a ha. and only eight-tenths of one percent were as large as 20 ha. or more, and most of these were in the Tihama area. Despite the very small size of farms, 80% were fragmented; two-fifths had 2 or 3 parcels[8] In the past, neither the small size of farms nor the extent of fragmentation appear to have had a negative effect on production, given the labor intensive methods of cultivation and the surplus of farm labor. However, with increasing mechanization, both size and fragmentation can be constraints to increasing output.

The current available data on tenure status in Yemen is mixed, if not confusing. The 1980 land tenure study undertaken by ECWA indicates that in the lowlands tenure arrangements were rather evenly distributed among owners, part owners, part tenants and tenants; while in the highlands about one-seventh of the farms were tenant- or part-tentant operated.[9] While the findings of the agricultural census in six provinces tend to be fairly consistent with the ECWA study for the highlands, there appear to be substantial differences with regards to the lowlands.[10] The census data show that for Hodeidah province, which lies mostly within the lowlands area, almost four-fifths of the farms are owner operated and slightly over four-fifths of the total land areas are owner operated. Similarly, the data for Taiz and Hajjah governorates, which are partly in the lowlands, show a high percentage of owner operators. While some qualitative work indicates tenancy is more prevalent in the lowlands than the highlands, the data on tenancy in the one district covered in the Airphoto project final report appear to indicate the results in the agricultural census may be closer to the mark.[11]

Traditional land tenure is adapted to subsistence agriculture and probably has a negative effect on production for the market. Changing the sharecropping arrangements described below would have a positive effect on investment and production by tenants.

The current practice of employing verbal lease contracts in the lowlands (69%), but written contracts in the highlands (60%) provide security to tenants, especially since the length of most leases is indefinite and tenants are usually permitted to retain the land if all obligations are met. Written contracts are preferred by both tenants and owners in the highlands in order to avoid future disputes, while in the lowlands custom and mutual confidence between owner and renter were the major reasons for verbal contracts.

The right to operate leased land after the tenant dies is inherited by family members. Although there is provision for the land owner to terminate leases under the present system, in such cases the tenant is compensated for farm improvements. Compensation is determined by community leaders or appointed arbitrators and strictly follows the customary practice in the locality. Changing share arrangements discussed below may, however, lead to some lessening of the tenant's security.

Most land is rented on a share crop rather than a fixed

amount basis. This is consistent with Islamic law which stipulates that a contract must be without major risk to both parties. Such an approach allocates risk to both the tenant and the landlord.

Sharecropping arrangements have been changing in recent years, as labor has become scarce. Whereas a decade ago it was common for tenants to receive shares between 25% and 33%, depending on such factors as region of the country, cropping patterns, water availability, cost sharing arrangements and size of parcel rented, tenants now often receive shares of 50 to 80%.

> Landowners in Jiblah declared that, whereas formerly '.... the land lord (malik) was prince, these days the sharecropper (sharik) is prince.'[12]

If tenant shares continue to increase, due in large part to alternate job oppportunities for sharecroppers, this may cause owners to seek out alternatives to current sharecropping arrangements such as greater mechanization and owner operation.

Up to the present the tenancy arrangements in Yemen appear to be working well, with increasing shares going to the tenant in recent years. The system's continuing evolution will be determined by the changing structure of agriculture from subsistence to commercial farming.

C.   Qat

Qat as an institution in Yemen is a complex social and economic issue.[13] The Yemeni in the highlands culti- vates the qat (Catha edulis) tree for its leaves, which are chewed to produce a mental high that increases alertness and creates a sense of euphoria, insomnia and anorexia. The leaves are chewed almost daily by at least three-fourths of Yemeni men, though considerably fewer women. Most chewing occurs in mid-afternoon, social qat chews, where men gather to talk, conduct informal business and visit. Qat is seldom chewed while a man is involved in agricultural work, but it is common in the afternoons to see merchants and taxi drivers with large wads bulging from their cheeks. Qat is not physically addictive and there is no firm evidence of major health problems.[14] Yemeni migrants do not chew qat in Saudi Arabia, where it is proscribed.

The production of qat during the past decade has increased dramatically. While there are no quantitative measures of the increase in land area, all observers in the YAR attest to the rapid expansion of qat cultivation. The MAF estimated that in 1981 between 40-45,000 ha. were devoted to qat.[15]

The increase in qat production is due to a sharp rise

in demand. While gat chewing used to be confined to those in the upper income levels, especially urban, it is now indulged by all segments of Yemeni society. Since gat is a relatively easy crop to produce in the highlands with its low production costs, low labor requirements and extremely high returns, many farmers have switched land over to gat. The quality and yield can be improved by irrigation, so many new pump-well gat farms have sprung up in the central plains in the last few years.

The marketing of gat is conditioned by several factors. First, the leaves are highly perishable and should be marketed within 24 hours. Second, branches of leaves are bulky and do not pack well. Third, since gat leaves are only picked a maximum of two times a year, it is necessary to stagger the harvest so that the market is not flooded. Nevertheless, there is a highly efficient marketing system that within a days transports the leaves from remote areas to urban and rural markets. This has only become possible with improved roads and use of pickups.

The farmer appears to receive about 80% of the retail price of gat, which ranges from about YR 40 ($9) a bundle to YR 150 ($33) for the highest quality. The farmer pays a 10% production tax (zakat) and there is a market tax of 10% paid by the dealers for marketing in urban areas such as Sanaa.

Increased use of gat has had a profound effect on

crop choice, patterns of food consumption, allocation of time, and investment in agricultural systems. It is obvious that land previously cultivated with food crops, particularly sorghum, has been switched to qat. Yet, high returns on qat help finance investment in pump wells or pickups that raise farm productivity and income. Although many new wells are primarily for qat irrigation, these also provide water for expanding food crop production, particuarly vegetables.

The effect of increased qat use on nutrition is difficult to assess. On the one hand, consumers may spend as much money on qat as on food for their families. This may reduce the available food money in poorer families, a particular problem for women and children. Qat is also an anorexic and reduces the overall food consumption of chewers. On the other hand, increased income from qat production allows farmers an opportunity for more income, which can be used to buy basic foods on the market.

D. Migration/Remittances

Migration from Yemen is of two types: long-term and short-term. Long-term migration has been going on for at least two hundred years to places as scattered as Vietnam, Indonesia, the Philippines, Europe, America, Ethiopia, and Somalia. The data inc   that recent long-term migration is declining, from 3   00 long-term migrants of 1970 to 175,000 by 1980. This discussion is not concerned with long-term migrants, but with short-term migrants who mostly work in the Arabian peninsula. This type of migration is a more recent phenomenon, probably starting about 25 years ago, but gaining impetus with the oil wealth revolution of neighboring states.[16] This migration and its accompanying flow of remittances have become institutionalized as an integral part of the social and economic fabric of the YAR.

There is no exact count of the number of short-term migrants and there is wide disparity among various counts and projections. By the same token the amount of remittances is determined by those officially recorded through the banking system plus a percentage factor for repatriation outside the system. This may be substantially underestimated.

The evidence indicates that at its peak in 1978 the number of short-term migrants did not exceed 500,000. Calculations based on population, remittance or other quantitative or qualitative data all support the half million estimate as a maximum. Officially recorded remittances have ranged from a low of just over YR 1 million in 1975 to over YR 6 million in 1978 and now are running around YR 4 to 4.5 million.

The institutionalization of short-term migration and remittances has engendered fundamental changes in the agricultural system. First, agricultural labor which had been in surplus, is now relatively scarce. Since the 1960s agricultural wages have increased 20 to 25 fold. As a result, it is no longer possible to use surplus labor to construct and maintain much agricultural capital, particularly highland terraces. Second, the flow of remittances into the country has changed the economy from a closed subsistence economy to an open market economy. Farm households now participate fully in the open market as consumers and increasingly as producers and investors. Third, the availability of income from remittances has greatly reduced the risks associated with rainfall or spate irrigated agriculture. Farmers have become less risk adverse in making investment and production decisions. Thus, the Yemeni farmer is able to be responsive to changes in market prices. Fourth, remittances have increased the level of capital investment significantly. At the village or subdistrict (uzla) level the local communities, either through LDA or on their own, have raised money to construct roads, schools, wells and clinics. Private investments by farmers have been in wells and irrigation systems, mechanical farm equipment, generators, trucks and plant material. Fifth, demand for agriculture products has expanded to cover a wide variety of products, while previously it had been confined largely to sorghum, a few vegetables and fruits, meat and milk products and herbs. This change in demand has caused farm production to shift toward producing a wide variety of crops both for on-farm consumption and the market.

E.   The Ministry of Agriculture and Fisheries

The MAF has been organized in its present form since 1970 under a Minister and his Deputy.   There are six sections known as General Administrations, which are Agriculture Affairs, Planning and Statistics, Financial and Administration, Livestock, Fisheries and Irrigation.   The General Administration of Agricultural Affairs has several Departments, including Agricultural Extension, Agricultural Machinery and Plant Protection and Plant Production, the latter including such things as agronomy and horticulture. There are also Provincial Agricultural Officers in each province who report directly to the Deputy Minister.   In addition two major rural development projects, SURDU and TDA, are directly supervised by the Deputy Minister.

To meet changing conditions, a proposed new organization for the MAF has been developed but not yet approved. Under the proposed new organization the Minister would be assisted by a consultant to the Minister and certain authorities would report directly to the Minister.   These include the TDA, ACB, the GCDFR and a new Agricultural

Research Development Authority. All agricutural research would be supervised and coordinated by the Research Authority. Under the Minister would be a Deputy Minister and two Vice Deputy Ministers. There would be a Vice Deputy for Finance and Administration and one for Technical Departments. The number of General Administrations would be increased from six to nine, the three new ones being Marketing Development, Extension and Training and Rural Development. Within the new structure the General Administration for Agricultural Affairs would have six branches: Engineering Crop Production, Plant Protection, Horticulture, Forestry and Agricultural Machinery. Finally, there would be ten provincial agricutural offices, the heads of which would report directly to the Minister. It is planned that all development projects would be placed under the authority of the provincial agriculture officers, who would be responsible for supervising and monitoring the projects. It must be recognized that shortages of trained personnel at all levels will make it impossible to adequately staff the ministry at all but the highest levels. Functioning of the MAΓ for the foreseeable future will continue to rely on expatriate assistance.

1. The New Extension Service

The proposed General Administration for Agriculture Extension and Training would be composed of five offices:

Extension Program, Training, Agriculture Information, Home Economics and Follow-up and Evaluation. In each of the provincial agricultural offices, there would also be an Extension department with three divisions: Extension Programs, Training and Home Economics. There would then be subordinate extension and training organizations at the district and village levels. Finally, the plan calls for a staff of Extension Agricultural Specialists in all program areas. They would work in the different offices and departments at national, province, district and village levels. They would also be expected to participate in follow-up and evaluation of extension activites.

Full implementation of the planned extension service must necessarily proceed slowly, because of staffing limitations. The extension service is woefully short of staff. Except for limited areas where there are rural development projects, it functions at a very low level or not at all. Extension centers were first developed during the 1974-76 period under the aegis of three rural development projects. A total of 36 centers have been developed in the vicinity of Hodeidah, Wadi Zabid, Ibb and Taiz. Training for extension agents at these centers has been carried out by the TDA and CARS.

The major problem in building a functioning extension service is the lack of trained people. The agricultural secondary school at Ibb is beginning to graduate students who will be available as possible extension agents and a second school at Surdud has started its first class. The development of an extension service which can provide useful services to farmers throughout the country is a very long-term proposition. It is unlikely that such a task could be accomplished within the next decade, although progress can be made. Promoting useful advice to farmers over the near term will probably require maximum utilization of the available modern communications systems which reach virtually all Yemeni farmers. This includes radio, television and video tapes. This can be supplemented by training courses for village leaders at research centers. It will need to be linked to the development of some system which relies on self-reliance and the participation of LDA and village or sub-district power networks.

2. Agricultural research

Prior to 1973 with the start of the UNDP Agricultural Research Project, there had been no agricultural research in Yemen. This remains the major research effort, but has been supplemented and duplicated to some extent by research carried out by various agricultural projects. These projects include: (a) the TDA, financed by IDA, which conducts research at Zadid and Surdud on a variety of field crops; (b) the Jarouba farm, where USAID finances research on tropical and subtropical fruits; (c) research on agronomy, forestry, animal nutrition, economics, and extension being financed by the British at Risabah; (d) research on animal diseases and mechanization being conducted by the British under the animal health project and the agricultural engineering project; (e) variety, fertilizer and other trials on potatoes being carried out by the Dutch at Risabah under the Rural Development Project; (f) research on fertilizer and pesticides at the German Farm in Shuub; and, (g) Chinese research on cereals and, other crops at El Butna, under a project financed through the MAF. In addition, planned activities are being considered for an IFAD-funded research station, a Japanese-funded research station in Hajjah, an FAO/World BAnk project in Wadi Jawf and a planned research station in Saadah.

In principle the UNDP/IDA/FAO Agricultural Research Service can coordinate all agricultural research in the YAR. In practice, however, there is little communication between the CARS and other researchers under specific donor projects. Efforts have been made to establish an informal research council including representation from all bilateral donors. This monthly meeting has thus far met with little success.[17]

The Agricultural Research Project will be moving into its third phase this year with financing by IDA, IFAD, Italy and the YAR. It will become the major vehicle for establishing the Research Authority already referred to in the discussion of the reorganization of the MAF. This project will cost $32.4 million and develop a research staff of 44 senior scientists, 49 junior scientists and an administration and technical staff of 121. Higher education will be provided only for professional staff at Ph.D. and M.S. levels. Under the first two phases of this project the ARS provides training for extension agents required for the TDA and Surdu. However, it is not expected that this extension training will be continued under the new organization.

Current and planned donor assisted research, particularly the new IDA project, appears to be capable of providing necessary research over the next five years. The one major requirement is coordination of research under the guidance of the new Research Authority.

3. Summary

The MAF and its components remain in a formative stage. The basic and fundamental institutional weakness at this time and for the immediate future is the scarcity of adequately trained personnel to staff the ministry at all levels of technical, professional and administrative staff. Strengthening the ministry as an institution requires the provision of adequately trained and experienced staff.

F. Agricultural Education

There are few opportunities to receive any education in agricultural subjects in the YAR. No agriculture is taught in the primary or regular secondary schools; nor is there an Agricultural College at the University. There are only three technical agricultural schools within the YAR school system: the Ibb Agricultural Secondary School, the Surdud Agricultural Secondary School and the Sanaa Livestock Secondary School.

1. Ibb Agricultural Secondary School

The Ibb school is just beginning its fourth year of operations with USAID assistance. The design capacity is 270 students or 90 per year, but functional capacity is probably closer to 60 per year. Enrollment has been about 55 in 1979, 23 in 1980, 32 in 1981 and 45 in 1982. Attrition within school is low, since 52 of the first 55 have graduated. This school offers a three-year agricultural course for training extension agents and other agricultural technicians. Graduates can also continue university agricultural studies. The major problems of the school are poor design and construction of buildings and the low enrollment, which is caused chiefly by the lack of adequate recruitment efforts among preparatory school graduates. An additional problem is the shortage of funds for farm operation and other current expenses.

2.   Surdud Agricultural Secondary School

This school started in 1981, with IBRD financing
expatriate staff salaries for four years. Although the
design capacity is for 180 students, enrollment has been
only 35 students in 1981 and 31 in 1982. The school offers
a three-year agricultural course for extension agents and
other technicians. The problems are similar to those of the
Ibb school, but Surdud suffers from shortages of library
books, laboratory equipment, audio-visual equipment, etc.

3.   Bir el Guhoum (Sanaa) Veterinary Secondary School

This school is financed by IBRD, including equipment
and staff salaries for four years and is scheduled to open
in November 1982. The design capacity is about 180 students
or 60 per year, but by October 1982 only about 20 students
had sought enrollment. The school offers a three-year
program, which integrates animal production and animal
health subjects to produce polyvalent animal husbandry,'-
veterinary technicians.

4.   Short-term Training

In addition to the institutionalized education
described above, there will be some short-term training, up
to one year, provided under various projects in extension,
veterinary and mechanization. This training will presumably
terminate when the projects terminate.

a.   SURDU/CARS Extension Agent Training

Since 1974, CARS has trained about 170 agricultural extension agents through eleven-month courses. About 90% of the graduates are recruited by SURDU and the rest by other rural development projects. About 70% of the graduates still serve in these projects, since the topping-off of MAF salaries by the projects is one incentive for continuity. Most of the rest have gone on to more advanced agricultural studies or to other positions which utilize their training. CARS also offers in-service refresher courses to the SURDU extension agents.

b.   TDA Extension Agent Training

The TDA also conducts eleven-month extension agent training in its Wadi Zabid facilities. Training is offered intermittently according to TDA requirements. About 150 agents have been trained so far. Annual one-week refresher courses are also offered.

c.   Veterinary Agent Training by the British Veterinary
     Services Project

About 100 animal health assistants have been trained since 1976 through seven twelve-month courses of the British Veterinary Services Project under MAF auspices. Twenty-one students are currently enrolled. Due to low demand, the school has to mostly admit students who completed primary school only. Attrition is about 30% and only about 50% of the graduates have joined the agricultural services, since many students use this school, which is conveniently located in Sanaa, as a stepping stone to higher and often unrelated studies.

d.   Agricultural Mechanics Training by the British Agricultural Engineering Project

The Yemeni-British-Agricultural Engineering Project has trained in the last four years about 20 mechanics per year in a one-year course in tractor repair. The trainees are mostly public sector employees. The project has recently started training SURDU extension agents through a one-month course in tractor operation and maintenance so they can instruct the farmers in these skills. By the end of 1983, all SURDU agents should undergo this training. The British project also upgrades rural mechanics through two-week courses.

Clearly agricultural education in Yemen is inadequate. Improvement at all levels is sorely needed, but priority needs are for technicians and B.S. graduates who can fill the middle level jobs so essential for providing services to farmers.

G.   Agricultural Credit

1.   Private Credit

Credit needs among farmers are not extensive, because of the inflow of remittances, although demand has increased during 1982. There are informal systems within villages for obtaining and providing credit, usually but not always, among people who have a kinship link. Because credit is usually provided by a wealthy person to a relatively poor person, it is not unusual for part of the loan to be repaid by the borrower working for the lender.

The World Bank has stated there is also private commercial agricultural credit av ilable at high interest rates.

> The traditional sources of agricultural credit in YAR have been merchants, large-scale farmers and, recently, private money-lenders whose effective interest rates are as high as 100%.[18]

Little is known about this private lending, but Yemeni farmers interviewed have said they knew no one who had recourse to this source of financing. It is difficult to reach any conclusion about the extent or importance of this private commercial credit system.

2. Public Credit Institutions

Institutional credit in Yemen was initiated in 1974 with World Bank assistance. An agricultural Credit Fund was established in the Central Bank to finance credit needs of farmers within a World Bank-financed Tihama project. In 1975 YARG established the ACB with an initial capital of YR 30 million to provide credit to Yemeni farmers, except those being assisted by Bank projects. In 1979 the NCDB was established to make loans to LDA and rural agricultural cooperatives. The government provided 60% of the capital and CYDA 40% for a total of YR 60 million. In addition LDA and cooperatives deposited YR 60.7 million between 1979 and the end of 1981.

In 1981 the ACF and ACB were integrated. However the new ACB faced liquidity problems, despite a paid-in capital of YR 100 milllion. It was forced to severely restrict short term loans to farmers during 1981. The problem stemmed from earlier loans of YR 85 million to a livestock company and a poultry company, plus an equity investment of YR 24 million in the poultry company. During the 1975-81 period ACB made about YR 65 million in medium-term and YR 35 million in short-term loans. Prior to 1981 repayment rates on ACB loans were about 95%, but in 1981 the rate dropped to 55%. During the 1975-81 period the ACB made loans in kind to farmers and consequently became a major supplier of farm machinery and fertilizer. ACB suffered an operating loss in every year but one from 1975 to 1981.

The situation in the NCDB was quite different. Until the end of 1981, the NCDB had made only two loans totaling YR 3 million. The NCDB actually operated as an overdraft facility for the LDA and had as much as YR 60 million on deposit with commercial banks at 9% interest, while it paid no interest on LDA deposits. The NCDB operated at a profit.

In January 1982 to ACB and the NCDB were merged to form

the CACB, which has an authorized capital of YR 300 million, of which 170 million is paid up. The new bank will make loans to farmers, agricultural cooperatives and LDA.

The World Bank is preparing a loan package of $12.7 million of which $5.5 million will be provided by the Bank, $2.2 million by the government and $5 million by an as-yet-unidentified donor. Of this amount, $6 million will be to furnish credit funds to the CACB with the remainder for technical assistance, construction and operating costs. The major focus of the Bank project will be to provide in-service training to the entire CACB staff and establish improved management, financial operations and information. Under the provision of the loan, the amount of loan guarantees and equity participation to any borrower will not exceed 10% each of unencumbered capital. Additionally the CACB will no longer sell farm machinery or equipment and will limit fertilizer sales to rural agents.

Assistance requirements of the CACB would appear to be met by the Bank project. The Bank does not anticipate any difficulty in finding another donor to furnish the additional financing required.

H.   Agricultural Cooperatives and the LDA

The first stage of the movement to establish cooperatives in Yemen was initiated by Yemeni writers in 1939. They dealt with the urgent need for establishing agricultural associations and called upon the government and rich merchants to help in implementation.[19] After the overthrow of the Imam in 1962, the government enacted a law providing for the establishment of cooperatives. The first cooperative was formed by Red Sea fishermen in 1964. In 1967 LDA was formed and established the main thrust of the cooperative movement in Yemen.

LDA are associations formed in a governorate, district or subdistrict for the purpose of carrying out projects benefiting the community. Initially LDA were local organizations formed and administered locally, without any centralized governmental authority. However, in 1978 CYDA was established by the YARG as the apex organization and central diverting body for LDA. From 1973 through October 1981, the following activities were undertaken by the LDA:[20]

Projects	Accomplished		Cost (YR)
Roads	19,505	km	810,085,227
Road Maintenance	6,000	km	48,000,000
Education	4,800	classrooms	244,934,789
Health	111	projects	22,278,997
Water	1,713	projects	157,662,953
Miscellaneous	343	projects	71,182

Quite obviously LDA are not agricultural or marketing cooperatives. They are community development associations which have contributed to agricultural growth by building up infrastructure.

The farmer cooperative movement in the YAR is small and limited. There are 42 cooperatives, all but one of which are located in the area immediately surrounding Sanaa or Hodeidah. CYDA is the apex organziation for the agricultural cooperatives, as well as the LDA. The major function CYDA performs is facilitating cooperatives' efforts to obtain credit, obtain assistance from the government, procure supplies and equipment, etc.

The functions of the cooperatives are to market crops, distribute farm inputs, build wells, and promote credit. Cooperatives can be formed by any group and are chartered by CYDA aftrer meeting certain conditions The cooperatives are run by an elected administrative committee and have the usual officers and committees. All members are required to purchase shares and pay dues. Members may own as many as five shares, but not more.

The farmer coocerative movement is obviously only getting started in Yemen, although there is a long tradition of cooperative help in Yemeni agriculture. The importance of cooperatives may increase with the commercialization of agriculture.

NOTES

[1] Cynthia Myntii, Women and Development in Yemen Arab Republic. Rossdorf, Germany: German Agency for Technical Cooperation, 1979, p. 32

[2] There are exceptions to these few generalizations. However, they are indeed exceptions and do not lessen the importance of the generalizations.

[3] Cynthia Myntti, Ibid., p. 59.

[4] Richard Tutwiler and Sheila Carapico, Yemeni Agriculture and Economic Change. Sanaa: AIYS, 1981,, p. 16.

[5] Myntti, Op. cit., p. 24.

[6] There are regional variations in the YAR, but this listing represents a generalized view for the highlands. For more information, see Myntti, Op. cit., p. 62. It must be noted that women in the Tihama region do virtuallly no agricultural work.

[7] Myntti, Op. cit., p. 62. Note that male day laborers often receive an even higher wage, if the cost of qat provided is considered.

[8] MAF, Department of Planning and Statistics, Summary of the Final Results of the Agriculture Census of Six Provinces, Ministry of Agriculture and Fisheries, Department of Planning and Statistics, Sanaa, YAR, 1981, Tables 4 and 7.

[9] Crop Sharing and Land Tenancy Practices in the YAR Report No. 1., 1980, p. 14.

[10] Ibid., Table 9

[11] H. Steffen, et al., Op. cit., p. II-84.

[12] Tutwiler and Carapico, Op. cit., p. 60.

[13] For a more complete discussion of qat in Yemen, see Daniel Martin Varisco, On the Meaning of Chewing: The Significance of Wat (Catha edulis) in the Yemen Arab Republic, Paper delivered at the annual MESA meetings, Philadelphia, November, 1982.

14 One exception to this is that _qat_ chewing by women
    reduces the amount and quality of breast milk.

15 IBRD, _Agricultural Sector Study_, 1981, p. 49.

16 World Bank, _Manpower Development in the Yemen Arab
    Republic_, 1981, p. 45.

17 IBRD, _Agricultural Sector Study_, 1981, p. 24.

18 World Bank, _Report and Recommendations of the
    President of the International Development Association
    to the Executive Director on a Proposed Credit in an
    Amount Equivalent to US $5.5 million to the Yemen Arab
    Republic for an Agriculture Credit Project_, October 1,
    1982, Project Summary, p. 11.

19 Abdelwahab El Muayyad, _Cooperative Movement in Yemen;
    Its Beginning and Development_, Sanaa, Yemen Arab
    Republic, undated, p. 5.

20 Working paper for Contributions of Yemen Cooperative
    Development Associations to the Second Yemeni
    International Development Conference.

V. AGRICULTURAL EDUCATION AND TRAINING

A. The Present Situation

Regarding the present situation of skilled agricultural manpower in Yemen, this report fully concurs with the IBRD assessment of the subject [1], which concludes:

> Effective manpower development continues to be a major constraint to development in the agricultural sector. The government still relies heavily on expatriate staff not only for the implementation of major investment projects but also for the direction of many of the normal services to agriculture. The replacement of expatriate staff by newly trained Yemenis as was anticipated in the three-year and five-year development cycles has not taken place. The need for more expatriate staff has expanded. Yemeni counterparts on most on-going projects have apparently not yet reached the stage of management competence to effectively take over the jobs of the expatriates. In general, the performance level of Yemeni staff is low. In all too few cases have qualified Yemenis been available to serve as project and program managers.

> The massive overseas training program launched during the First Five-Year Plan should provide enough trained people to meet most of the requirements in the Second Five-Year Plan (SFYP) for professional level cadre, given more attractive working conditions and salary scales. Inadequate supply of technical level cadre has actually been the most serious bottleneck to the implementation of the foregoing development activities and stands to be even more serious in the SFYP.

B. Skilled-Manpower Projections in Agriculture to 1986

The supply and demand for skilled agricultural manpower may best be reviewed in the context of total demand for skilled manpower in Yemen. The present report is fortunate in being able to draw on the recent CPO projections [2] which are based on a complete census of all public-sector institutions and on GDP growth/productivity estimates for the private sector. The results are shown in Table V-I. The table indicates that during the period 1982-86 the surplus of unskilled workers will grow by about 98,000 persons, while the deficit in all categories of skilled personnel will grow by about 196,000 persons. The projections show that the most serious deficit will be in the lower skill categories: semi-skilled workers (deficit = 93% of the additional demand) [3], skilled office workers (92% of demand) and skilled manual workers (81% of demand). [4] Only slightly less serious will be the deficits among university-level and subprofessional liberal-arts graduates, 67% and 64% respectively. The demand in these categories is created mostly by the need for Yemeni teachers. The deficit among subprofessional science graduates will be 66% of demand. Interestingly, the least serious deficit will be in the category of scientific univeristy-level professionals, i.e., 14% of the additional demand. Earlier and less detailed IBRD projections [5] generally agree with the above estimates.

The supply-and-demand situation for skilled agricultural manpower parallels the general situation

discussed above. The professions requiring university training that are most essential for agricultural development are
those of irrigation engineers, agronomists, horticulturalists and veterinarians. In all of these occupations,
Table V-1 shows the additional supply over the period
1982-86 to equal the additional demand. In other words, if
all the students training for these occupations successfully
terminate their studies at the expected time, return to
Yemen and be immediately employed in their chosen
professions, no deficit will be created. The extent of
shortfall which is bound to occur in practice is thus equal
to the combined effect of the university dropout and
repetition rates, delays in return to Yemen due to pursuit
of advanced degrees or work experience abroad, delay in
finding jobs and employment in other occupations. Dropout
rates for agricultural students studying abroad

> are estimated at more than 70% mainly caused by
> students changing their fields of specialization
> and/or failure to pass their courses or seeking
> jobs in other countries when they have
> successfully completed their studies.[6]

If this trend continues, the shortfall in these three
employment categories will be 70-78% for overall
agricultural graduates at the B.S. level.

CPO and MAF records show that 518 students were sent
abroad through 1981/82 for university-level agricultural
studies. Of these students, 80% were sent to

Egypt, Syria and Saudi Arabia, 10% to other Middle Eastern countries, 7% to Eastern-Block countries and 3% to the U.S. Table V-2 shows that most of the demand for agronomists and veterinarians is generated by the MAF including SURDU, TDA and bilateral projects, but that for professions such as irrigation engineer and economist demand is largely outside the MAF.

The liberal-arts professions most important for agricultural development are those of economists and accountants. For economists the projected deficit is only 15% of the additional public sector demand. For accountants, the projected deficit is 61%. Only 7% of the demand for accountants originates in the agricultural sector, mostly in the ACB and NCDB.

At the subprofessional level, the occupations relevant to agricultural development are those of laboratory technicians and veterinary assistants. As no training is programmed in these occupations at that level, the deficit is 100%. The numbers of persons required, 29 and 7 respectively, are small.

Considerable deficits are projected for bookkeepers/cashiers (76%) and stock clerks (93%), who are necessary for agricultural credit and inputs management. The agricultural sector demand for these occupations is a small part of the total demand.

At the technician level, a demand is projected for 664 agricultural technicians, chiefly extension agents, and 120 livestock technicians. Compared with the projected outputs of the agricultural vocational schools, the above demands signify deficits of 64% and 17% respectively.

Another important demand in the agricultural sector is for skilled manual workers, including skilled mechanics capable of providing maintenance on agricultural machinery. The projected deficit for all skilled manual workers in the total YAR economy is 81%. It is reasonable to assume that the shortage of mechanics who can work on agricultural machinery is similar to the overall percentage shortfall of skilled manual workers. The current wage rate of YR 40-80 per hour for diesel mechanics would tend to confirm that there is a shortage. However, there are no data on the number of mechanics needed, so it is difficult to estimate training requirements.

CPO estimates put the total employment in the agricultural sector in 1981 at 830,400 persons or 69.1% of the total economically active population of 1,201,600 persons. By 1986, the agricultural labor force is expected to grow to 886,735 persons, but its share in the economically active population of 1,420,843 will diminish to 62.4%. Most of the surplus of unskilled labor during the SFYP, estimated at about 98,000 persons (Table V-1, will be

in the agricultural sector. This indicates the importance
of upgrading unskilled rural workers to the semi-skilled and
skilled levels, in order to mitigate the deficit of about
63,000 semi-skilled workers projected during the SFYP (Table
V-1), and in order to prepare Yemeni workers to compete
better in the labor market of the Gulf States.

C. Agricultural Education and Training

Agricultural education and training institutions and
projects within Yemen have been described in Chapter IV,
where it was noted that no university-level agricultural
education is available in the YAR. The need for in-country,
university-level agricultural training has been established
by previous studies. Reports for FAO[7] and AOAD, recommended a four-year curriculum with five specializations:
crop production, horticulture, animal production, agricultural engineering and agricultural economics and extension.
Initial enrollment would be between 30 and 60 students per
year, with a tentative future target figure of 150 students.
A study mission from Yemen to Jordan, England and the U.S.
recommended constituting the faculty on a modified land
grant college model[8]. Present plans are to start studies
in October, 1983, and have the first graduation in 1987.
Financing for construction has been promised by Iraq.

Institutionalized training at two agricultural

secondary schools can be expected to produce between 85 to 120 agricultural technicians per year, although some of these will probably go on to university education rather than immediately joining the labor force. The Bir el Gurkoum school will probably produce 20 or more veterinary assistants per year by 1985.

In addition to this institutionalized education, short term training of one year or less is being provided under a variety of projects. Since 1974 about 320 extension agents have received eleven months of training under the SURDU and TDA rural development projects. Two British financed projects have provided training in animal health and mechanics. Over a period of seven years about 100 Yemenis have completed one-year training as animal health assistants. Over four years 80 mechanics have completed a one-year course in tractor repair. The Agricultural Mechanics Training project also provides short courses of one month and two weeks for extension agents and rural mechanics. These project training courses will last as long as the projects continue, but they will not provide skilled or semi-professional training over the long haul.

In addition to education training within the YAR, a substantial number of Yemenis receive agricultural education at the university level in foreign countries. CPO and MOE records show that through 1981/82 about 518 students were sent abroad for university level agricultural studies. However, IBRD reports that between 1974 and 1981 some 788 students were sent abroad, 65 for studying veterinary science. The World Bank reports that only 30 of the 338 students who should have returned to Yemen had been employed by MAF as of October 1981. This indicates that only 9% of the students returned to take up employment in the public sector. However, if one uses MOE records which show fewer students going abroad during the 1974-77 period than the IBRD data, the percentage of students returning to take up public sector employment was much greater, about 75%. An average of these two return rates is 39%, not too far off the 30% return rate cited earlier in this chapter.

Education is lacking at all levels within the agricultural sector. This is as true at the farm level as it is at the senior science level. Illiteracy is widespread throughout the country, averaging 80% or more. This means that many people are unable to use written information, whether it explains fertilizer applications, tractor maintenance or the proper mixture for infant feeding preparations[9]. Improvement of human capital at the farm level through increased literacy and associated skills at all age levels is essential for the effective utilization of new technology and investment capital.

The opportunity for any Yemeni to receive education or training, particularly in agriculture, is extremely limited. As indicated above, no agriculture is taught at the primary or secondary school level, except for two agriculture and one veterinary secondary schools. At best these schools altogether could not provide technical agricultural education for more than 540 to 630 students at any one time. Vocational schools and basic skills training centers of the MOE teach little that is useful to the agriculturalist. Extension agents providing training for farmers are limited to specific projects supported by foreign donors. Education of extension agents, other than the specialized training provided within projects, is limited to that provided by the Ibb and Surdud schools. Some 500 to 700 students have gone abroad with the intent of studying agriculture at the undergraduate or graduate level. Yet it is uncertain how many will return over the next decade to take up positions within the agricultural sector. Within Yemen there are no agricultural education opportunities above the secondary level.

D.   Strategic Considerations

Because the education and training needs are so pervasive, choices are difficult to make; yet, because resources are limited, choices must be made. In setting priorities the multiplier effect of alternative strategies becomes the most important criterion. First priority must therefore be accorded to providing education for those who will provide education and training services to others in the agricultural sector. Second priority would then be for those who would provide non-education and training services to agricultural producers. As output of professional, technical and skilled personnel from the first two priorities begins, additional resources will need to be devoted to expanding education and training in the skills and knowledge essential for the farm family as a producing and consuming unit.

Within this overall strategy it is then possible to identify specific kinds of educational and training needs. Education at two levels produces personnel who provide both priority one and priority two services. Agricultural education at the B.S. level produces graduates who can not only educate and train others but also provide the necessary administrative and management skills needed for the successful operation of schools or training institutions such as an extention service. Graduates are also capable of providing services such as veterinary, pest identification or soil testing to farm operators. Finally, it is from the B.S. pool that students move on to graduate school to become the senior agricultural scientists. Agricultural secondary schools produce middle level technicians who can function as extension agents providing training to farm families and as technicians in such fields as agricultural mechanization and animal husbandry. Thus, within the framework of this strategy, first priority in agricultural education and training would be given to B.S. and graduate levels of education. This will produce graduates who can provide services and also provide necessary administrative and scientific leadership. Second priority would be for middle-level, technical, secondary education.

Many services needed by farmers are provided by skilled and semi-skilled workers such as mechanics and blacksmiths. As capital investment continues to increase in such things as tractors, trucks, diesel pumps and generator, the demand for these kinds of services rises dramatically. In order to increase possibilities for maximum utilization of capital investment by farmers and to minimize capital wastage, third priority would be given to training skilled and semi-skilled workers in selected fields.

As investments in the first two priority areas begin to produce results, the YARG will want to move quickly to assure that educational and training services provided to farmers are rapidly expanded. This includes literacy and skills training related to agriculture, as well as extension training in improved cultivation practices and new technologies. This will necessarily proceed more slowly than anyone will desire, because of scarce financial and personnel resources. However, there are possibilities for speeding up farmer education and training through the use of mass media. This approach seems particularly appropriate in Yemen where radios, TV and video cassettes are found even in the most remote villages. Much can be done to generate and broadcast agricultural information through imaginative programming.

NOTES

1   IBRD, <u>Yemen Arab Republic - Agricultural Sector Analysis</u>. November, 1981.

2   D.A. Siddiqui and S. Ghawi, <u>Human Resources Needs Assessment Survey in the Yemen Arab Republic for the Second Five-Year Plan Period</u>. CPO, Sanaa: CPO, 1981.

3   Deficit in this context means positions which are filled by inadequately qualified persons, occupied by expatriates or remain vacant.

4   The highest percentage deficits are in those skilled at semi-skilled occupations which require the largest number of workers. This accurately reflects the absolute shortage of training facilities at all levels.

5   IBRD, <u>Manpower Development in the Yemen Arab Republic Report No. 3181a</u>, March 27, 1981.

6   M.A. Taha and A. Banaga, <u>Faculty of Agriculture. University of Sanaa. Consultant Report</u>, FAO, 1982, p.3.

7   M.A. Taha and A.M. Banaga, <u>Op. cit.</u>

8   CID/FAPU, <u>Findings and Recommendations as a Result of the Study and Observation Tour by the Faculty of Agriculture Planning Unit (FAPU)</u>, Oct. 1981.

9   It should be noted that many illiterate farmers have access to someone in the village who can read.

TABLE V-1
ADDITIONAL MANPOWER SUPPLY AND DEMAND FOR AGRICULTURALLY-RELATED
OCCUPATIONS IN THE PUBLIC AND PRIVATE SECTORS
1982-1986

Group[a] and Occupational Classifications[b] / Occupation	Additional Demand, 82-86	Expatriates in 1981	Total Additional Demand 82-86	Additional Supply 82-86	Surplus (+)	Deficit[c] (-)	Surplus or Deficit as % of Demand	Sources of Addi-tional Supply[d] Local	Foreign	Local as % of total
A-1 Professional-scientific Total public Sector	1857	427	2283	1708	-	575	-25%	204	1595	11%
0-22 Civil Engineers	201	45	246	246	-	-	-	10	236	4%
0-53 Agronomists, Horticul-turalists, etc.	487	31	518	518	-	-	-	16	502	3%
0-65 Veterinaries	18	4	22	22	-	-	-	-	22	-
Total Private Sector	815	295	1111	1187	76	-	+ 7%	48	1048	4%
Total group A-1	2672	722	3394	2895	-	499	-14%	252	2643	9%

continued/2

TABLE V-1

ADDITIONAL MANPOWER SUPPLY AND DEMAND FOR AGRICULTURALLY-RELATED
OCCUPATIONS IN THE PUBLIC AND PRIVATE SECTORS
1982-1986

Group[a] and Occupational Classifications[b] Occupation	Additional Demand, 82-86	Expatriates in 1981	Total Additional Demand 82-86	Additional Supply 82-86	Surplus (+)	Deficit[c] (-)	Surplus or Deficit as % of Demand	Sources of Additional Supply[d] Local	Foreign	Local as % of total
A-2 Professional-arts										
Total public sector	7850	842	8692	2002	-	2290	-26%	1486	516	74%
0-90 Economists	249	22	271	229	-	42	-15%	176	53	77%
1-10 Accountants	1318	150	1468	576	-	892	-61%	280	296	49%
Total private Sector	532	592	1124	1226	102	-	+9%	1201	25	98%
Total group A-2	8382	1434	9816	3228	-	6588	-67%	2687	541	84%
B-1 Subprofessional-scientific										
Total public sector	2567	1255	3822	1219	-	2603	-68%	1219	-	100%
0-54 Laboratory technicians	260	9	269	-	-	269	-100%	-	-	-
0-66 Veterinary assistants	7	-	7	-	-	7	-100%	-	-	-
Total private sector	1423	358	1821	721	-	1100	-60%	721	-	100%
Total group B-1	4030	1613	5643	1940	-	3703	-66%	1940	-	100%
B-2 Subprofessional-arts										
Total public sector	2501	1403	3904	2302	-	1602	-41%	2302	-	100%
Total private sector	2786	72	2858	122	-	2736	-96%	122	-	100%
Total group B-2	5287	1475	6762	2424	-	4338	-64%	2424	-	100%

TABLE V-1

ADDITIONAL MANPOWER SUPPLY AND DEMAND FOR AGRICULTURALLY-RELATED OCCUPATIONS IN THE PUBLIC AND PRIVATE SECTORS 1982-1986

Group[a] and Occupational Classifications[b] Occupation	Additional Demand, 82-86	Expatriates in 1981	Total Additional Demand 82-86	Additional Supply 82-86	Surplus (+)	Deficit[c] (-)	Surplus or Deficit as % of Demand	Sources of Additional Supply[d] Local	Foreign	Local as % of total
C-1 Skilled office workers										
Total public sector	30186	8644	38830	8102	–	30728	– 79%	8102	–	100%
3-31 Bookkeepers and cashiers	3490	65	3555	869	–	2686	– 76%	869	–	100%
3-91 Stock clerks	525	28	553	36	–	517	– 93%	36	–	100%
Total private sector	66298	358	66656	–	–	66656	–100%	–	–	–
Total group C-1	96484	9002	105486	8102	–	97384	– 92%	8102	–	100%
C-2 Skilled manual workers										
Total public sector	4245	104	4349	2162	–	2187	– 50%	2162	–	100%
6-11 Agric. technicians	664	–	664	240	–	424	– 64%	240	–	100%
6-12 Livestock technicians	120	–	120	100	–	20	– 17%	100	–	100%
Total private sector	18260	2425	20685	2471	–	18214	– 88%	2471	–	100%
Total group C-2	22505	2529	25034	4633	–	20401	– 81%	4633	–	100%

TABLE V-1

ADDITIONAL MANPOWER SUPPLY AND DEMAND FOR AGRICULTURALLY-RELATED
OCCUPATIONS IN THE PUBLIC AND PRIVATE SECTORS
1982-1986

Group[a] and Occupational Classifications[b] Occupation	Additional Demand, 82-86	Expatriates in 1961	Total Additional Demand 82-86	Additional Supply 82-86	Surplus (+)	Deficit[c] (-)	Surplus or Deficit as % of Demand	Sources of Additional Supply[d] Local	Foreign	Local as % of total
D Semi-skilled workers										
Total public sector	2706	63	2769	2705	-	63	- 2%	2706	-	100%
Total private sector	62435	2425	64860	2006	-	62854	- 97%	2006	-	100%
Total group D	65141	2488	67629	4712	-	62917	- 93%	4712	-	100%
E Unskilled workers										
Total public sector	9154	48	8202	8154	-	48	- 1%	8154	-	100%
Total private sector	150988	2425	153413	251371	97958	-	+ 64%	251371	-	100%
Total group E	159142	2473	161615	259525	97910	-	+ 61%	259525	-	100%
Grand Total	363643	21736	385379	287459	97910	195830	- 25%	284275	3184	99%

Key for Occupational Groups

A1 Professional occupations presumably requiring a science-based university degree.
A2 Professional occupations presumably requiring an arts-based university degree.
B1 Subprofessional occupations presumably requiring 1-3 years post-secondary science-based education.
B2 Subprofessional occupations presumably requiring 1-3 years post-secondary arts-based education.
C1 Skilled office occupations presumably requiring 9-12 years of general education plus job training.
C2 Skilled manual occupations presumably requiring 5-10 years of general education plus vocational training.
D   Semi-skilled occupations presumably requiring functional literacy plus job training.
E   Unskilled occupations presumably requiring no special education.

a   For group classification see key.
b   According to 1900 classification.
c   Posts which will be filled by expatriates or by inadequately-trained persons or remain vacant.
d   Yemenis returning from training abroad.

Source: CPO

115 D

TABLE V-2

MANPOWER DEMAND FOR AGRICULTURAL OCCUPATIONS IN THE PUBLIC AND MIXED SECTORS, BY INSTITUTION

GROUP A1 AND OCCUPATIONAL CLASSIFICATION B1	OCCUPATION	STOCK IN 1981	ATTRITION 82 - 86	ADDITIONAL DEMAND 82 - 86	TOTAL DEMAND 82 - 86	STOCK IN 1986
A-1	Professional - Scientific					
0-22	Civil (Irrigation) Engineers	118	3	198	201	316
	MAF	5	2	50	52	55
	CYDA	2	-	9	9	11
	Coop. Bank	1	-	1	1	2
	Others	110	1	138	139	248
0-53	Agronomists	240	11	476	487	716
	MAF	110	10	286	296	396
	ARDA	13	-	44	44	57
	CYDA	4	-	7	7	11
	Coop. Bank	3	-	-	-	3
	Others	110	1	139	140	249
0-65	Veterinaries	5	-	18	18	23
	MAF	4	-	17	17	21
	Others	1	-	1	1	2
A-2	Professional - Arts					
0-90	Economists	80	2	247	249	327
	MAF	1	-	26	26	27
	ARDA	-	-	5	5	5
	CYDA	-	-	6	6	6
	Coop. Bank	-	-	1	1	1
	Others	79	2	209	211	288

continued/2

TABLE V-2

MANPOWER DEMAND FOR AGRICULTURAL OCCUPATIONS IN THE PUBLIC AND MIXED SECTORS, BY INSTITUTION

GROUP A1 AND OCCUPATIONAL CLASSIFICATION B1	OCCUPATION	STOCK IN 1981	ATTRITION 82 - 86	ADDITIONAL DEMAND 82 - 86	TOTAL DEMAND 82 - 86	STOCK IN 1986
1-10	Accountants	1054	23	1295	1318	2349
	MAF	7	-	17	17	24
	ARDA	1	-	3	3	4
	General Seed Authority	8	-	10	10	18
	CYDA	3	-	3	3	6
	ACB	44	-	42	42	86
	Coop. Bank	36	-	17	17	53
	Others	955	23	1203	1226	2153
B-1	Subprofessional - Scientific					
0-54	Laboratory Assistants	110	-	260	260	370
	MAF	-	-	9	9	9
	ARDA	-	-	20	20	29
	Others	110	-	231	231	341
0-66	Veterinary Assistants	19	2	5	7	24
	MAF	19	2	5	7	24
B-2	Subprofessional - Arts					
3-31	Bookkeepers & Cashiers	2286	90	3400	3490	5686
	MAF	10	2	80	82	90
	ARDA	3	-	2	2	5
	General Seed Authority	13	-	10	10	23
	CYDA	4	-	-	-	4
	ACB	14	-	6	6	20
	Coop. Bank	18	-	40	40	58
	Others	2224	88	3262	3350	5486

115 F

continued/3

TABLE V-2

MANPOWER DEMAND FOR AGRICULTURAL OCCUPATIONS IN THE PUBLIC AND MIXED SECTORS, BY INSTITUTION

GROUP A1 AND OCCUPATIONAL CLASSIFICATION B1	OCCUPATION	STOCK IN 1981	ATTRITION 82 - 86	ADDITIONAL DEMAND 82 - 86	TOTAL DEMAND 82 - 86	STOCK IN 1986
3-91	Stock Clerks	655	144	381	525	1036
	MAF	6	2	95	97	101
	General Seed Authority	5	-	4	4	9
	CYDA	2	-	-	-	2
	ACB	3	-	2	2	5
	Others	639	142	280	422	919
C-2	Skilled Manual Workers					
6-11	Agr. Technicians	84	20	644	664	728
	MAF	84	20	644	664	728
6-12	Livestock Technicians	-	-	120	120	120
	MAF	-	-	120	120	120
8-43/8-49	Mechanics	510	7	456	503	1006
	MAF	8	3	30	33	38
	CYDA	4	1	4	4	8
	General Seed Authority	9	-	7	7	16
	Others	489	4	455	459	944

Source: CPO

VI. HORTICULTURE

A.   Overview

1.   Fruits

a.   Demand and Production

There is an increasingly strong demand for fruit in the YAR. A major portion of the fruit consumed is imported, but with the exception of grapes, virtually none is exported. Apples from France and the US, bananas from the Philippines and Central America, oranges from Morocco and Brazil and almonds from Syria are examples of imported fruits found throughout the YAR, even in remote villages.

The value of major imports of fresh fruits in 1979/80 was $34 million for apples, $23.5 million for bananas and $14.5 million for oranges. This amounted to increases over the previous year of 81% for apples, 36% for bananas and 40% for oranges.

Actual volume of fruit production in the YAR, with the exception of grapes, is extremely small. Grape production was 64,300 MT in 1981 and that of all other fruits only 80,700 MT. Moreover, even though land area devoted to fruits, other than grapes, increased over 200% in the 10 year period from 1970-81, the amount of land involved is small and new land planted in the last several years has declined to an annual growth of less than 1000 ha.

On the other hand, there was a definite and significant rise in demand for fruit during the decade of the 1970's that has been attributed to: (1) the rate of population growth; (2) the growth in disposable income; and (3) the relatively high-income elasticity of demand. Prices for all fruits are high, but even higher prices are paid for locally produced fruits; price differentials are not related to quality as conventionally measured.

In brief, the demand and prices for fruits are strong. Production, with the exception of grapes, is far below the demand.

b.   Production Practices

The plant material used is, with a few exceptions, very poor from a genetic and/or disease standpoint. Government nurseries, from which most material is disseminated, are themselves repositories of damaging nematodes, virus and other diseases, insects, mites and a conglomeration of random genetic material. Some trees are imported from foreign nurseries without the safeguards needed. A recent shipment of citrus from Egypt was found to be infested with the citrus nematode (Tylenchulus semipenetrans), but these trees were not destroyed despite recommendations that this be done.

The most rudimentary professional horticultural practice worldwide now is to produce fruit tree and vine varieties true-to-type by budding and grafting on to rootstocks and using cuttings, layers, off-shoots, specialized underground stems and other vegetative means. However, in the YAR nurseries, deciduous fruits and nuts, with the exception of grapes, figs and pomegranate, are propagated with seed taken from inferior seedling trees, which produce fruit with generally inferior size, quality and yield.

A litany of malpractices in the propagation of citrus, mangos and other fruits can be documeted, but it suffices to say growers are charged atrociously high prices for inferior nursery stock. This inferior stock is often placed in mixed garden-type plantings that are crowded and virtually uncared for. Others are spaced in a reasonable orchard form and given some attention. However, overall management and cultural practices are clearly inadequate.

Despite the inferior planting material and lack of proper cultural practices, the production of fruit is highly profitable, primarily because of high prices paid for fruit and the preference for locally produced products.

It would be difficult to determine with any accuracy how much increased production could be obtained from existing plantings given proper care. In the case of most deciduous tree fruits and nuts the genetic material is so limiting that a large investment in improved cultural practices appears inappropriate. A modest investment in fertilizing, pruning and pest control might increase net returns, while better water management is badly needed to reduce production costs. Grapes, the most profitable and highly productive of all the fruit crops, for example, could be produced more economically, as there is evidence of excessive irrigation and inadequate, but expensive pest control. At least some planting of certain crops such as limes, oranges, mangos, bananas and papayas could benefit economically from better care. A considerable investment is justified, because genetic material of these crops is better than that of deciduous tree crops.

2. Vegetables

a. Demand and Production

A relatively narrow range of vegetables has been grown in the YAR over the years, but this was concentrated in the Tihama and urban areas. These vegetables include hot peppers, tomatoes, potatoes, garlic, onion, white radishes and chive. A wide variety of vegetables had not been part of the diet, thus, there has not been the same strong demand for vegetables as for fruits. There is little importation of fresh vegetables, but appreciable quantities of canned tomato paste and beans are brought in.

Demand for a wider variety of vegetables has expanded recently with increasing income and changing tastes brought about by migration. Farmers, with the assistance of several donors, have responded by increasing the quantity, quality and variety of vegetables produced.

Potato production has increased from 55,000 MT in 1971 to 138,000 MT in 1981, while production of all other vegetables has gone from 100,000 MT in 1971 to 290,000 MT in 1982, almost a threefold increase.

The YAR is largely self-sufficient in fresh vegetables and has started exporting a small amount of okra and tomatoes to Saudi Arabia. A tomato paste factory is under construction in Hodeidah, although its economic validity is questionable.

b. Production Practices

Most vegetable production is limited to small irrigated terraced plots in the Central Highlands, and Southern Lowlands. They are cared for almost as large gardens. Pest control and general care are reasonably good. This is due in considerable part to the work of the Federal Republic of Germany Plant Protection Program which has distributed seeds and seedlings of improved and new vegetable varieties, as well as trained extension workers in pest control and other cultural practices. The Netherlands Technical Assistance program has been equally effective in improving potato production.

3. Stimulant Crops

a. Qat

Qat (Catha edulis), which is native to Ethiopia, is a woody shrub or small tree grown extensively in the YAR at 800 meters elevation and above. Immature qat leaves are chewed daily by the great majority of the adult male population and by many adult females. There is an apparently insatiable demand for qat that has resulted in extensive new plantings and extremely high prices.

Qat is easily propagated from suckers and stem cuttings. It can be grown without irrigation, but responds well to it. There are no major pests and even fertilization is uncommon. Some growers feel qat is overplanted, but profits are easily three to four times that of any other cash crop. There seems to be little possibility that qat will cease to be highly profitable in the near future, although supply may outstrip demand in a few years, since the first crop can be obtained only three years after planting.

b. Coffee

Yemen grows an Arabica coffee that is still exported, but has no special qualities that would command a higher price than the Arabica grown elsewhere. Production costs are high, however, local demand for bean and husk is strong and rising, leading to prices that are above world levels, and reasonable returns from existing trees. Coffee also demands irrigation and suffers from a number of pests. Minor element deficiencies, especially iron, are common, due to the high pH of the soils in the YAR.

The outlook for coffee looks somewhat bleak, due to qat, which is easier to produce, gives an earlier return on investment and is more profitable on the same land.

B. Future Needs and Potential

1. Fruit Crops

Despite the poor state of existing nurseries and a large portion of the plantings, the basis of a productive, prosperous fruit industry exists. The technology for developing nurseries with appropriate sanitary and production techniques can be directly transferred internationally. The necessary genetic material, with some exceptions, is readily available for purchase. Assuming no undue administrative or financial constraints and the proper personnel, excellent nurseries and nursery plants could be developed within three to four years.

Establishing and maintaining good commercial and farm orchards is another matter. The YAR is both blessed and cursed with a wide variety of climates ranging from purely tropical through subtropical and temperate zone types. The various microclimates have not been identified. In the case of many deciduous fruit and nut varieties, it will be necessary to match deciduous fruit varieties having specific dormant season temperature requirements with an appropriate microclimate. However, the genetic material of certain fruit species, such as apples and peaches, appropriate for Yemeni conditions, is readily available for introduction.

The tree growth, fruit quality and yield of citrus fruits are also related to climate, but areas exist in the YAR in which high yields of excellent quality citrus can be produced. Some of these climatic zones are known; others will need to be identified.

Tropical fruits are less of a problem. Much of the genetic material in the YAR is inferior, but good genetic material can be imported into large, readily identifiable land areas in which tropical fruits such as mango, guava, papaya and banana can be produced. FAO is addressing this matter and, to a lesser extent, so is CID. There are also other tropical fruits, such as avocados and lychees, that are not yet established in the YAR, but should do very well in certain locations. Certain crops demanding low pH soils, such as pineapple and blueberry, can not be economically grown, even though there are suitable climates for them.

2. Vegetable Crops

The potential for production of high quality vegetables is tremendous, assuming availability of sufficient water. Virtually every vegetable existing can be produced somewhere in the YAR. Excellent farm gardens can be developed throughout the YAR, greatly adding to the nutrition and variety of diet of the rural populace, as well as to farm incomes.

The Tihama has vast areas that could produce huge quantities of watermelons, as well as many other kinds of melons, tomatoes, eggplants, okra and storage onions. The area lends itself to mechanization, which could overcome to some extent the high cost of labor, thereby opening the prospect of producing large crops for export to the fresh markets in Jeddah and Riyadh by the new coast road.

Many of the same crops could be grown in season in the cooler climates of the Southern and Central Highland regions. The cool season crops, such as cabbage, brussel sprouts, cauliflower, lettuce and various other leafy vegetables, could be grown in large quantities in these regions, as could potatoes.

There is, of course, the continuing need for research, extension, education, and regulatory work. However, there is as much effort in these fields as can be absorbed in the YAR at this time.

3. Stimulant Crops

There is no question but that qat will remain the most profitable crop for some time. The potential for coffee is less optimistic. Local demand is growing rapidly, and foreign markets are no longer as attractive, as world prices fall. However, returns on qat are so attractive that growers will continue to plant qat in place of coffee, barring a dramatic reversal in comparative production costs and prices for coffee and qat respectively, which is unlikely.

C.   Donor Organizations

There are numerous donor organizations which impact on horticultural crops in some manner, but a few are of particular importance.

1.   The World Bank and associated donors have contracted with FAO to assist the MAF in developing a series of research centers that will include extensive applied research programs on horticultural crops. This is an extension of an existing, limited program which has functioned well. FAO is also executing a separate coffee production project designed to enhance the profitability of coffee through improved production practices and a project to reduce the spoilage of fresh produce through proper handling practices.

2.   The Federal Republic of Germany Plant Protection Project for Field Crops, which includes vegetables, fruit crops and coffee, provides support to the Plant Protection Department of the MAF in its pest control work. It trains Yemeni staff and farmers in pest control practices,

maintains plant protection machinery in a workshop, screens
pesticides, conducts research and advises the MAF on
registration of pesticides and plant quarantine. It raises
vegetable seedlings that are distributed to farmers and has
sold thousands of knapsack sprayers and pesticides to
farmers at nominal cost. It also has five high-volume
sprayers, and thousands of knapsack sprayers which are
loaned to small farmers. In cooperation with the MAF, it
publishes a plant protection bulletin and a series of other
extension bulletins.

3. The Netherlands Technical Assistance Program Seed
Production Center is involved in all aspects of improvement
of certified potato seed. This includes working with local
farmers producing potato seed, demonstrating improved
cultural practices, training technicians, supervising
quality control and construction of cold storage facilities.
The project has been very successful.

D. Serious Program Deficiencies

1. Direct Transfer of Technology

a. The major constraint to fruit production is the lack of
fruit trees of the best genetic material, free of virus
diseases, damaging nematodes and other pests, on proper
rootstocks when applicable, and at a reasonable price.

b. There is a crucial need for development of quarantine
measures and their enforcement to prevent the entrance of

pests affecting fruit crops. Without such enforced quarantine regulations, much of the value of good nursery trees will be negated and the nurseries themselves endangered.

c.   Another problem is the use of proper cultural practices, such as spacing, pruning and fertilizing.

2.   Research

There is a lack of knowledge of the microclimates of the Central Highlands and the Southern Highlands and the influence of the geography associated with these microclimates. This knowledge is needed if fruit varieties with definite climatic requirements are to be matched with the appropriate microclimate.

3.   Extension Service

There is a lack of an effective, well-organized extension service and of adequately educated persons to absorb the technological training needed.

4.   Education

The lack of a college of agriculture at the University of Sanaa, the only university in the YAR, is a deficiency that prevents the YAR from absorbing the information and assistance in horticulture being extended by donor agencies.

E.   Strategic Considerations

1.   Research

Vegetable production, including potatoes, has increased

considerable in quantity, quality and variety over the past decade. Research and direct technology transfers related to these crops are now being adequately covered by donor assistance. The most important requirement is institutionalizing this capability within the MAF. While there are no significant research deficiencies on the production side, additional work on market development is required.

2. Nurseries

The demand for fruit crops is strong and large quantities of fruits that could be economically grown in Yemen are imported. The major factor limiting fruit production is the use of plant material that is genetically inferior and contaminated with disease and pests. Inferior material is also being imported and supplied by government nurseries. The development of model nurseries of deciduous and tropical fruit trees produced from mother plantings of the best genetic material, both imported and domestic and free of budwood transmitted diseases through use of efficient nurseries techniques, is the single most important requirement in the field of horticulture.

The model nurseries should produce large quantities of the highest quality trees for sale by the MAF at reasonable prices, supply government nurseries with mother trees and other propagating material and train government nurserymen and nursery inspectors. The nursery program would include testing scion varieties and rootstock of imported materials, as well as selecting superior strains of local material. Such a program will be successful only if directed by highly qualified staff supported by adequate financing.

3. Plant Protection

The Federal Republic of Germany Plant Protection Project is developing quarantine laws and regulations with the YAR Plant Protection Agency. The quite comprehensive FAO program for developing a series of research centers and a national research program contains extensive research projects that include a wide range of research on fruit and other horticultural crops. Extension is just now being organized on a national scale, but donor organizations are training or assisting in training of extension agents in subject matter fields; however, no field of work is ever covered completely. Thus, any additional research, extension or plant protection work, including quarantine in horticulture, should take into account work already underway and coordinate with it.

VII. DRYLAND AGRICULTURE AND IRRIGATED FIELD CROPS

A. Overview of Dryland Agriculture and Irrigated Field Crop Production in the YAR

About 90% of the land area of the YAR produces either cultivated crops or native range forages; the remaining 10% is in rock outcropping or other land not usable for agriculture. Of total land area, about 15% is potentially tillable, and an estimated two-thirds of this is cultivated for crops at any one time. Of this cropland, 85% or more is rainfed, the balance utilizing some degree of supplemental irrigation. The grains (sorghum, millet, wheat, barley, and maize) have traditionally occupied about 90% of all cultivated land. Sorghum, and to a much lesser extent, millet are the predominant grain crops representing about 80% of total grain production. A substantial part of the sorghum and millet is interplanted with pulses, primarily cowpeas and mung beans. Their use has been divided between grain, for human consumption, and leaves, stalks and roots used for livestock feed and fuel. During the past few years there has been some shift away from grain to crops of higher value, particularly qat, vegetables and fruit crops.

Most of the dryland cropping is on mountain terraces, plateaus and in valleys or in the Tihama coastal plain. Because of the low level and lack of dependability of rainfall in the Tihama, much of this area is planted with millet.

1. The Role of Range and Forage in Mixed Crop and Livestock Production

Although in eastern Yemen there have been Bedouin herders who graze the rangelands with their herds, most agriculture has been of a settled nature. The farmers in the villages have used the grain crops as their staple source of food. Animals are kept for meat, milk, hides, wool, dung, draft power and transport. Although there are rapid changes taking place, this traditional system still remains more or less intact at the present time. When the rains arrive and the land produces new growth, the small stock are herded onto the range, mostly by the children and old men. The range, which is the predominant land use in the YAR, provides feed for the animals while the crops are growing. At the end of the rains when the range has stopped producing new growth and existing feed has been consumed, the animals are brought back and fed on the leaves stripped from the stalks of the ripening sorghum or maize. After the grain is harvested, the upper stalks with the remaining leaves are saved to provide feed for the animals until the rains arrive and start the sequence over again.

a. Condition and trend of native ranges

The system of range use described has been taking place

for centuries without consideration for the management practices required to maintain the range in good condition. As a result, essentially all ranges in Yemen are in poor condition with minimal ground cover. Over the centuries this has resulted in severe soil erosion that has left most rangeland with nearly all the soil mantle eroded away to predominantly rock subsoils. Fortunately, man-made terraces utilized the water run off to capture and retain much of the soil eroded away through poor management of the ranges in mountain areas. Unfortunately, the poor condition of the ranges eliminates their effectiveness as a watershed-regulating device to retard runoff, allow water to soak into the soil to feed springs and recharge groundwater. The resulting rapid runoff causes destruction of terraces, loss of soil, siltation of waterways and serious flooding on a more frequent basis. This deterioration has been further enhanced by the elimination of the forests that once covered the higher slopes in the higher rainfall areas. The limited amount, quality and low fertility of the soils left on much of the rangeland makes restoration of adequate range condition and afforestation extremely difficult.

(1) The Tihama

The natural forage cover of this coastal plain is particularly vulnerable because of the low rainfall, frequent droughts and low water holding capacity of many of

-132-

the soils   Lack of proper grazing practices has resulted in large areas of shifting dunes devoid of any vegetation. These dunes cause serious sand and dust storms that damage crops and drift over roads, dwellings and other structures. The end result is increasing areas of desertification that can only be stopped through major programs of dune stabilization, by planting of windbreaks and seeding new groundcover.   Unless grazing practices are changed, such efforts, however, may be futile.

(2)   The Southern Highlands

This is the highest rainfall region in Yemen and the ranges have the highest yield potential and ability to support forest cover. Because of the higher rainfall, the range is of maximum importance as watershed.   Currently the ranges are in poor condition and there are no remnants of previous forests.   There is indication though, of recent reduction in grazing pressure from the considerable seed formation of grasses and other species that would not be expected with consistent overgrazing. This would indicate a significant recent reduction in animal use of most grazing lands, caused by sizeable reductions in animal numbers or much greater confinement of animals to the immediate vicinity of villages.

Because of the higher potential of the highlands for both forestry and significant range production, this area would be the natural priority area for initial improvement efforts.

(3) The Central Highlands

The vegetation remaining in this area is sparse, but adequate for recovery under proper range management practices. With the much lower rainfall and cooler winter, total production potential is limited. The watershed value of ranges in this region is very high and range improvement is of major importance to the potential for sustaining agriculture. The same evidence of significant recent decreases in grazing pressure noted for the Southern Highlands was also quite evident in the Central Highlands.

2. The Use of Food Crop Residues For Livestock Feed

There is a high demand throughout Yemen for livestock feed and a ready market for any surplus crop residues that can be fed to livestock. In general, the straw, leaves and stalks of grain crops, pulses and the residues of other crops generate higher returns per ha. than the grain or seed.

a. Sorghum, Millet and Maize

The farmers tend to select varieties of these crops as much on fodder yield as they do for grain. If drought causes failure of grain to mature, the crop can still be harvested for feed. Where conditions are favorable for good grain yield, the leaves of the growing maize and sorghum plants are stripped up to the few top leaves when the grain reaches the soft dough stage. The leaves are either dried for future feed or fed green. This practice might reduce both the yield and quality of grain, but income may be increased because the leaves have a very high value as animal feed when alternative feeds are scarce and animal producers command a high price.

After the grain is harvested, the entire upper portion of the stalk is cut to provide feed until the ranges again start growing. The lower portion of stalk and roots are eventually pulled and dried for use as fuel.

b. Wheat and barley

These grain crops are cut or hand pulled about the time the stems are losing most of their green color. The sheaves of grain are dried and then threshed. The remaining straw is used for animal feed and has a high cash value, so varieties with high straw yields are preferred. The return per ha. on straw is usually greater than on grain.

c. Pulses

Much of the sorghum, millet and maize is intercropped with cowpeas or mung beans. In addition, lentils, fenugreek, dry beans, and peas are raised either alone or intercropped. If they set a good seed crop, they are threshed and the residue fed as fodder; but, when seed set is poor, the whole plant is used for animal feed.

d.   Other crop residues

Any crop residue readily consumed by livestock is utilized for this purpose. This would include cull potatoes, the tops of many of the vegetable crops and the residues of oil seed and industrial crops such as sugar cane, sesame, etc.

3.   Forages Grown for Feed

The recent high prices for animals and the associated high value of animal feed has caused increased planting of high yielding forage crops.

a.   Alfalfa

In the higher rainfall areas and on farms with some irrigation, alfalfa is a very desirable forage crop. It is cut in the partial-to-full-bloom stage and sold green in 2 kg. bundles for YR2, the equivalent of about $220 per ton green weight. Since the yield on a green-weight basis can reach 15-25 tons per ha., gross returns range from YR15-25,000 per annum. It provides a high quality supplement to the basic low-protein livestock feed ration.

b. Sudan grass, maize and sorghum

The high price for quality animal feed has stimulated increased production of Sudan grass and silage type maize and sorghum varieties. They provide high quality feed which is lower in price and quality than alfalfa, but much superior to fodder left after grain harvest. This type of

crop can only be grown in higher rainfall areas or where
supplemental irrigation is available.

c.   Other forages

CARS is conducting promising trials on various forages,
including legumes and grasses.   These new introductions are
in the test stages and have not yet found their way into
significant use.

4.   Food Grain Crops

a.   Sorghum, millet and maize

Sorghum and millet have been the traditional basic food
grain crops in Yemen and they still make up 80% of grain
production.   Hectarage planted with sorghum and millet has
decreased by about 30%, but higher yields have limited
output decreased to about 15%.   Where sufficient water is
available, there has been a switch from sorghum and millet
to qat, fruits, vegetables, and maize.   More marginal
rainfed land has gone out of production in almost all parts
of the YAR.   Maize production increased one-half during the
FFYP period, but it is still less than 10% of total grain
production.

(1)   The Tihama region

Nearly all the millet is grown in this region, because
low rainfall makes sorghum a high-risk crop.   Millet is
often planted with a pulse crop, and no prior tillage, if
there has been enough rain to give reasonable assurance of

adequate soil moisture to produce a crop. It can be planted on dunes and in areas with reasonable soil depth. If it does not receive have enough moisture to mature grain, it will be cut for animal feed. Very little work has been done on variety or cultural improvements until very recently. Recent research initiated on millet by the TDA and CARS has given promising indications for improved yield. Varieties introduced from ICRISAT show considerable promise for yield improvement.

In the Tihama, sorghum and maize are limited to irrigated conditions. Research on new varieties and cultural practices for both sorghum and maize have been promising. These crops give high returns in grain and fodder and are competitive with other crops.

(2) The Central and Southern Highlands

In both of these regions sorghum is by far the predominant grain crop. The growers prefer tall growing varieties with large amounts of leaves and large heads to maximize both grain and fodder yields. They have been very successful over the years in selecting varieties that are well adapted to each local microclimate, providing high yields of grain and fodder of desired quality. The major problems affecting sorghum are high incidence of smut diseases of the head and various leaf diseases. Attacks by stem borer and other insects frequently cause major damage,

-138-

and substantial grain is lost to birds in all regions of the country. Efforts to develop varieties with improved yield potential and greater resistance to pests and diseases had been carried out in 1977-81 by Arizona State University. Similar work for the Southern Highlands and the Tihama has been done by CARS. Significant progress has been made in indentifying new varieties with higher yield potentials and greater pest resistance. However, researchers should not pursue increased grain yield at the expense of lower fodder production. In fact, farmers might prefer the opposite given the high value of fodder and the ubiquity of imported grain.

Both CARS and GT% have shown that seed treatment greatly improves stands and eliminates smut diseases. Use of pesticides and fungicides to reduce stem borers, other insects and leaf diseases has been shown to be cost effective when properly used.

Maize improvement work by CARS has led to the identification and release of high yielding varieties and improved production practices. The high yield potential of maize in the higher rainfall areas under supplemental irrigation is leading to rapid increases in production.

b. Wheat, barley and triticales

Wheat and barley have been grown for centuries in the highlands. The barley is used primarily for bread; and therefore, the predominant varieties are of the two-row naked grain type. The area planted in barley has declined in recent years due to the increased availability of imported flour wheat and an urban preference for wheat bread. Farmers will continue with barley in areas where its lower moisture requirements and tolerance of cool weather make it preferable to other grains. There has been recent research by CARS on variety improvement, indicating that a switch to naked grai six-row head types can improve yield.

With rising incomes, wheat consumption has increased in Yemen. This has led to substantial increases in imports and interest in increasing domestic production. As a result, CARS has initiated substantial wheat improvement work and has identified a number of varieties with substantially improved yield potential. Although the total demand for wheat probably makes attainment of self-sufficiency impossible, improvements in production potential from research should lead to some increases in output.

c. Pulses

Most of the pulse crops are intercropped with the grains. Cowpeas and mung beans are the primary pulses, followed by dry beans, fenugreek, lentils and peas. Mung beans and cowpeas are used for food and livestock feed. CARS has initiated testing of pulse varieties developed by various international research centers. It has introduced chickpeas and pigeon peas from ICRISAT that show considerable promise. Because these crops all fix nitrogen, they are soil-improving and make excellent crops for interplanting or as rotation crops with cereals. The work on these crops can benefit from association with the USAID-financed global project on Nitrogen Fixation of Tropical Legumes based in Hawaii.

5. Industrial Crops

None of the industrial crops are grown without supplemental irrigation. There are some oil-seed crops that require minimal water and may be grown without irrigation in the higher rainfall areas.

a. Cotton

There are large areas of deep fertile soil along the various wadis that are being developed for irrigation in the Tihama and are well suited for cotton production. The YAR needs about 30,000 tons of cotton per year to fill domestic requirements. A few years ago cotton was Yemen's largest export but low prices, coupled with serious damage by termites and other pests, caused a drastic drop in production. Research by TDA and CARS has solved most termite and pest problems. The introduction of improved varieties and production practices along with improved prices and credit availability may bring about some increase in cotton production. Such an increase is likely to be short lived because current price and production cost relationships greatly favor other crops over cotton.

b. Oil Seed Crops

Sesame, the primary oil-seed crop is largely used for confectionary rather than for oil extraction. Consumption of edible oil in Yemen is increasing rapidly and is totally dependent on imports. Physical conditions appear favorable to production of several oil seeds. CARS is currently testing sesame, sunflower, safflower, peanut and soybean varieties. One variety of peanut from ICRISAT has shown unusually high yields in tests in the Tihama where soils are ideal for this crop. Excellent results have also been obtained in the Tihama with irrigated sunflower. Safflower has given acceptable yields under dryland conditions in the higher rainfall areas of the highlands. These crops, however, cannot complete in net returns per ha. with fodder, fruit and vegetables grown for the local market. Like cotton, oil-seed prices are kept low by abundant supplies on the international market. In Yemen, net returns to farmers are likely to be higher for other crops, and oilseeds of the higher value, confectionary type might be more acceptable to farmers.

c. Sugar Crops

Sugar is a major import into Yemen. A small amount of sugar cane is grown but sold as confectionary, not for processing into sugar. CARS has experimented with rainfed sugar beets for the higher rainfall areas with marginal success. Sugar production in Yemen is not viable, because of the scarcity of water and sugar's low price on the international market.

B. Future Needs and Trends

1. Soil Conservation and Sand Dune Stabilization

Unless the uncontrolled runoff from denuded ranges in the highlands can be overcome, there is increasing risk of extensive deterioration of the terrace system and downstream flood damage. The control of increasing desertification in the Tihama is a prerequisite to sustained development of the region.

a. Terraced Central and Southern Highlands

The deforested and denuded condition of the rangelands in this region has already been discussed. A large portion of the crop production in these regions is based on an extensive system of terraces built over the centuries to utilize and retain the soil washed off the rangelands and to systematically harvest the water as it comes down the mountains. Recent developments have greatly reduced labor availability and increased the cost of adult male labor

which traditionally maintained these terraces, thus putting
the whole system in jeopardy. There is substantial evidence
of terraces in good condition being abandoned where the
soils and rainfall are marginal. Ominously, one sees
terraces washed out by floods. This tends to have a domino
effect on all terraces below, because the system is based on
a careful channeling of runoff from terrace to terrace down
the hills. Each broken link puts greater strain on the
terrace below. Failure of a terrace system dumps a heavy
silt load in the runoff that finds its way to downstream
areas. This chokes stream flow and makes water diversion
systems inefficient or ineffective through rapid siltation.

Overcoming these problems calls for a comprehensive
range management and afforestation program. The high value
of animals, fuelwood and construction poles makes the
economics appealing over time. At the present time MAF does
not have either the staff or capacity to develop the
necessary strategy, policies and implementation plans. This
is an area that is very difficult to implement and in which
progress is slow. At present there is only a little donor
assistance activity in developing forest tree nurseries and
pilot test plantings. The ARDA will have a small range and
forestry research component, but this appears inadequate in
face of the need.

b. Tihama

The problem in the more arid Tihama region is stopping the extensive shifting dunes that are the main vehicle of increased desertification and destruction of the agricultural potential. This is a problem common to a number of areas in Africa with similar climatic and soil conditions. Dune stabilization methods have been worked out; the main requirement is their implementation in Yemen, plus controlling grazing practices to prevent repetition of the problem. Limited donor assistance is being provided. The UNEP has expressed willingness to coordinate a donor program, once the MAF has been able to develop the prerequisites. This implies prior ministerial capability which is lacking at present.

2. Tillage Practices

During the last fifty years there has been increasing research in many of the low rainfall areas of the world on the best tillage methods to conserve moisture, minimize erosion and optimize yields. This has led to major changes in tillage/weed control practices, resulting in dramatic improvements in dryland agriculture productivity. The traditional tillage methods in Yemen are those that the new practices have replaced in other countries. The only current ongoing activity is limited work under the Farm Mechanization project at Taiz. Unfortunately, plans for the

FAO Phase III ARDA project do not include either tillage or weed control activities. Issues relating to the advantages and disadvantages of tractor ploughing, particularly on the right type of ploughs, are particularly pressing.

3. Use of Modern Inputs

Improving the agricultural productivity of dryland crops requires a package of improved inputs. These include high quality seed of improved varieties, proper seed treatment, correct seeding rate, adequate soil fertility, pest control by chemical and biological means and careful soil and water management to maximize the efficiency of rainfall or water applied by irrigation.

a. Improved varieties

Varieties with improved yield potential and pest and disease resistance are being developed in many research stations located in areas with similar climatic conditions. The fairly comprehensive program of research established by CARS, which will be expanded by the implementation of ARDA starting in January 1983, has been effectively testing the new varieties developed throughout the world. This is a very appropriate approach. Specific breeding programs are justified only where introduced materials have special problems which can only be overcome through breeding. Once better varieties have been identified, their impact on production is dependent on an adequate farmer-level demonstration/testing program, systematic maintenance of genetic purity, and a seed production organization which ensures both seed purity and quality. An effective extension system is needed to demonstrate the new varieties to farmers and provide them with the necessary package of inputs. An FAO Seed Improvement project has established the basic seed increase and distribution system with the necessary processing and seed testing facilities. The extension requirements are being handled on a limited basis by extension programs under TDA and SURDU. There is also support to plant protection by GTZ, more limited extension support from the British Mechanization project and from rural development projects assisted by the Peoples Republic of China, and The Netherlands. The major limitation is the lack of a comprehensive national extension service.

b. Mechanization

The increasing shortage and price of agricultural labor are forcing mechanization on the larger size farm holdings. This is being backstopped by funds available through the CADB and by British technical assistance. The real gap is in adequate development and introduction of appropriate machinery and methods to convert to improved dryland conservation, tillage and seeding methods.

c. Fertilizer

The dryland areas are deficient in both major and minor plant nutrients. The requirements are being studied by CARS and various projects are establishing fertilizer demonstrations. Fertilizer is readily available and lack of extension, not funds appears to be a limiting factor in its use. One problem is the extreme diversity of soils and climate throughout the country that would require an enormous soil testing and advising program to determine the greatest efficiency in fertilizer use. These capabilities do not currently exist.

d. Pesticides

Pesticides are readily available at reasonable prices. The limitation is inadequate information on their use at the farm level. The GTZ has a major and effective program to help develop the Plant Protection Service of MAF for this purpose. Until there is a well trained national extension service, the safe and effective use of pesticides will be handicapped. CARS has a substantial research program to develop the best recommendations for pesticide use as part of an input package for each of the major crops.

e. Water management and irrigation

The major limitation on crop production in Yemen is lack of adequate water. As already indicated, better tillage and weed control practices are needed for the dryland areas. Water use under irrigation is inefficient, excessive and wasteful. Adequate programs to correct these deficiences are not present or planned for the immediate future but deserve the highest priority.

4. Research

The establishment of ARDA to be operative in January 1983 will eventually create the network of research stations, trained staff and on-farm testing needed to backstop the agricultural needs of Yemeni farmers. The technical assistance to be provided by FAO during the first five years appears to be both comprehensive and the maximum that can be absorbed during this time frame.

5. Extension

The lack of a comprehensive national extension service is a major limitation to rapid adoption of the new technology already coming out of CARS. To overcome this difficulty, CARS has been training extension personnel assigned to two regional development projects in an eleven-month training program and assisting them in demonstrating new technology through a network of extension centers. This training will not be included in the new ARDA that replaces CARS. This increases the need to implement the national extension service which has been planned by MAF with World Bank assistance.

6. Education, Training, and Human Resource Development

All of the development activities discussed under dryland agriculture are currently dependent on expatriate staff and donor assistance. To staff the research network under ARDA will require a cadre of Ph.D. and M.S. level technical staff trained abroad. An even larger number of B.S. and technical high school level technicians will be needed as support personnel. Until such time as there is a local B.S. program in agriculture, these B.S. staff will need to be trained abroad. The Ibb and Surdud technical schools will need to train adequate numbers to provide the technicians required. There will be similar and parallel needs for the national extension service.

Although all the formal needs outlined are urgently required, rapid agricultural change will be dependent on developing the skills and knowledge of the men, women and children who actually do the farming. Because of the long time frame needed to develop a comprehensive extension network down to the village level, intensive effort should be devoted to alternative approaches. The CARS research program which already has eight years of development behind it, is producing new technology faster than it can be extended. With the high degree of television and radio ownership in even remote areas of Yemen, a skilled utilization of these mass media could overcome some of the lag in developing a traditional extension service. The high level of illiteracy in the countryside, particularly among women, precludes effective use of print media for many extension needs, although such people usually have access to someone who is literate.

C. Strategic Considerations

1.   Research

Considering the limited resources in both finance and trained staff, the research program started under CARS and being expanded under ARDA appears to be soundly conceived. It represents the maximum level of effort that can be absorbed, when taken in conjunction with specialized research undertaken within various donor financed projects. The main gap appears to be on tillage and weed control for dryland farming. It would also seem that certain USAID and USDA resources could be of help in these areas.

2.   Education and Training

There appear to be as many fellowships available for advance degree training as could possibly be utilized. There is less adequacy of fellowships to increase the pool of B.S. holders through training abroad until a local faculty of agriculture can be developed. There is an acute shortage of technically-trained, high-school, level graduates, the new facilities at Ibb and Surdad should soon start the process of overcoming the worst of this deficiency. Ultimately all training requirements are dependent on rapid improvement in elementary and secondary education throughout the country.

3. Extension

The gaps in extension have already been covered in previous sections. In addition to public sector activities, there is a need for policies that will encourage extension assistance by the private sector, as the distribution system for inputs and marketing and processing operations develop more fully.

4. Regulatory Requirements

This is an area of serious weakness in governmental institutional capacity. There must be the capacity to implement the plant quarantine law recently passed, to pass and implement pending pesticide legislation and to be able to formulate and enforce standards for seed and plant material, product grades and quality standards, including insect infestations, rodent and other unsanitary contamination. Development of these activities will require time, but planning and required training should be initiated now.

5. Input Availability and Distribution

In general, most of the inputs are readily available and, except for tractor spare parts and maintenance, reasonably priced. This is due both to private sector competition and efforts of the ACB to ensure adequate supplies were available to borrowers. As the need increases, too much government intervention could prevent the necessary level of private sector development to ensure ready supply and competitive pricing.

6. The Rangeland

Rebuilding the range grass, bush and woodlands to serve livestock feed, fuelwood supply, water and soil conservation purposes must necessarily be a long term endeavor. There are many difficult technical, social and economic issues that must be identified, analyzed and resolved. Initial efforts should be focused on building the institutional capability within the MAF necessary for developing, in cooperation with the farming community, feasible programs for rebuilding the range.

7. Grain Storage

Changes now underway in the Yemeni economy are leading to increased commercialization of grain production and consumption. As this trend continues, the requirements for on-farm grain storage will be modified. Storage requirements on the farm are likely to shift from holding grain over a number of years as a hedge against crop failure to short term storage of grain which will enable farmers to take advantage of fluctuating prices. At the same time increased marketing of domestically produced grains and continuing imports of grains will augment the need for adequate storage and distribution systems. The government should focus its major effort on developing the rules, regulations and services which will assure that the private marketing system services the needs of individual consumers and the nation.

VIII.   LIVESTOCK AND POULTRY

A.   Current Situation of Livestock in YAR

1.   Livestock Role

Livestock raising in Yemen is practiced almost entirely by traditional farmers. Accordingly, we find that crop production and livestock are closely interrelated. This clear link can be seen through the use of the fallow land, utilization of crop residue, animal involvement in crop production as a major source of draft power and, in some cases where green fodder and grains are fed to animals, competition for land and water. Besides providing food and draft power, livestock also represents a means for accumulating wealth and balancing the risk of crop failure in bad years.

Generally speaking, livestock has a complementary role to crop production, using available feed in the vicinity of the farm. To achieve this fully, farms keep different types of livestock with different grazing habits and requirements.

Cattle are mainly kept for milk, ghee, meat production and draft power. Sheep and goats primarily provide meat. Sometimes both ewes and does are milked about two months following suckling. Camels and donkeys, besides their use as draft animals, provide transport in traditional Yemeni society.

2. Livestock Population and Distribution

It is very difficult to give an accurate estimate of livestock population in Yemen. The available official figures are confusing. The 1976 estimates indicate that the livestock population was 3,460,000 sheep and goats and 800,000 cattle. The 1981 estimates show the number of sheep and goats to be about 3.8 million, while the cattle number was about 906,000. The camel population is about 60,000 and donkey 40,000. Owner attitudes, as well as technical problems will always make it difficult to get accurate estimates.

Based on impressions and various facts, rather than statistical data, one can conclude that there was a reduction in the livestock number in Yemen over the last 15 years. Such an assumption can be supported by the following facts:

a. The droughts of 1967/69 and 1972/74 forced many farmers to decrease the number of livestock.

b. The outbreak of rinderpest during 1976 and the lack of any animal disease control service caused a further major reduction.

c. Increasing demand for locally produced meat and shortage of supply caused a large increase in meat prices, which stimulated increasing off-take from the herds. This increase came from herd reductions and not from increasing productivity.

Based on observation and discussions with different experts involved in livestock, one can say that more than 45% of the livestock population is concentrated in the coastal Tihama region, with the bulk of it found in the irrigated areas. Another 30% is concentrated in the Ibb and Taiz provinces of the Southern Highlands. Table VIII-1 shows the official number of each major species of livestock owned by agricultural holders.

TABLE VIII-1

LIVESTOCK OWNED BY AGRICULTURAL HOLDERS[1]

Livestock Species	Dhamar	Hodeidah	Hajja	Mahweit	Taiz	Ibb	TOTAL
Cattle	108,933	119,150	93,904	35,939	170,166	192,365	720,457
Sheep	335,539	279,807	144,105	32,513	147,313	198,529	1134,806
Goats	139,559	180,768	120,847	20,977	179,855	147,601	789,636

3. Animal Husbandry Practices

According to official statistics, about 80% of the agricultural holders owned cattle, with an average of 2.2 head in reported holdings and 1.8 head in all holdings. Twenty-four percent of the reported holders owned sheep, with an average of 11.1 head for holdings reporting sheep, but 2.8 head when averaged over all holdings. About 20% reported goats with an average of ten head or an average of two head for all holdings. Depending on holding size, forage availability and available children and women, most farmers tend to have a small number of one or more species of livestock.

Women always take care of the cows, while men take care of oxen and children are mainly responsible for sheep and goats. In many areas, cows are usually kept in the house and hand fed sorghum or millet stalks chopped and wrapped in green fodder, most often alfalfa or green sorghum leaves. Sometimes cattle, especially lactating cows, are fed whole or store-damaged grain. In some locations, like the Tihama, cattle graze with sheep and goats on fallow land and crop residue. Sheep and goats graze together within the boundaries of villages mainly on fallow land, but this is always supplemented with straw.

The mating of cattle in most rainfed areas takes place after the rains. When heat is detected, the farmer usually takes his cow to the bull for service. Calf suckling is almost eight months. Goat and sheep mating can be seasonal depending on feeding condition, but it is generally after the rains. Sheep are rarely milked, mainly because of their low yield. Goats may be milked for one to three months after kidding. Most of the male lambs and kids are sold off at three to four months.

B.   Current Situation of Poultry Production in Yemen

There is a high demand for poultry products in Yemen. Statistics indicate that in 1980 imports of frozen broilers made up 50% of the total value of licensed imports of live-stock and poultry products. At the same time, broiler production is growing at a fast rate. Local broiler production has increased fourfold over the last four years, stimulated by high profits from consumer willingness to pay premium prices of 50-100% for locally produced, live chickens. In the case of egg production, consumer preference for local eggs is not so high, with the premium being only 20-30%. This, plus the complexity of egg production from the management and nutritional viewpoints, the high risk involved and the long cycle for cash turnove , are major factors making investment in egg production less attractive than investment in broiler production.

All large-scale broiler farms, both government and private, are based on highly sophisticated modern technologies; medium and small size farms are less modernized. All required feed and almost all needed pullets and hatching eggs are imported. Some large farms have imported parent stock and begun producing their pullets locally. Those who have hatcheries in Sanaa face low hatchability problems due to the high altitude; hatcheries should be sited at altitudes below 1,000 m.

C.   Livestock Development Projects

The objective of the FFYP was to increase livestock production in Yemen in order to narrow the gap between increasing demand and short supply. The main approaches to achieve this were:

-   introducing modern livestock production practices

    through establishment of modern dairy, finishing

and poultry farms;

-   improving animal health services;

-   introducing high yielding dairy breeds;

-   establishing meat markets and slaughter houses;

-   improving range land productivity.

The two major projects are a Livestock Credit and Processing Project and a Veterinary Service Project. Other rural development projects, such as TDA and SURDU include livestock activities.

1.   Livestock Credit and Processing Project

This project was designed to address all the issues related to livestock development other than animal health. It comprised operating units which have mainly administrative and service functions and the following four operating divisions:

a. Municipal Slaughter House and Market Division. The key objective is to develop the meat market infrastructure in main towns and improve skin and hide quality.

b. Livestock and Range Improvement Division. The objectives are to develop research on grazing systems and to demonstrate improved range management practices in ten village development centers.

c. Dairy Production Division. The objectives are to increase milk production through establishing eight 100-cow dairy farm units and to develop milk colonies in the villages.

d. Livestock Finishing Division. The objectives are to increase meat production and to demonstrate viability of modern fattening techniques.

The scope of the project activities has undergone many changes and limitations. The project has established a 72-cow dairy unit, a sheep finishing farm, a range improvement center and three village range centers.

As a result of inadequate logistical, manpower, land and financial inputs and unrealistic objectives, the project achieved little toward accomplishing its objectives, but will continue in the SFYP.

2. Veterinary Service Project

The project objective is to develop a national animal health service. It comprises a diagnostic laboratory, a training center and three field centers. The project has contributed considerably to reducing the effects of rinderpest, and in training veterinary attendants to do diagnostic work. The project will continue during the SFYP.

Although they are not yet finalized, most of the proposed projects in the SFYP are mainly governmental production projects based on improving foreign cattle fed on irrigated forage.

D. Constraints to Livestock Development

1. Forage Constraint

The principal constraint to livestock development in Yemen is lack of forage. The inadequate quantity and the quality of the available forage will always restrict the number of animals held by any agricultural holder.

The growing demand for livestock products cannot be met from increased domestic production under the prevailing situation, in which forage comes only from the fallow land, crop residue, weeds and canal banks in irrigated areas. Small areas are cultivated for forage, mainly alfalfa in the highlands and sorghum in the Tihama. Expansion in cultivated forage can only be achieved by competing with high-value food crops for high-priced arable land. Up to now, food crops have had top priority, though sorghum is grown for both grain and fodder.

The productivity of the scattered rangeland is very low

and its ability to supplement farm produced forage is very limited. Most of the range has been subjected to long-term deterioration as a result of deforestation, soil erosion, over-grazing or a combination of all of these factors. The present land tenure system also restricts access to range outside of tribal boundaries, even if not used by those who have the traditional right to graze it.

Crop production is not developed to the extent that a fodder surplus is produced. The small amount available for animal feeding is very expensive. The availability of oil-seed cakes or grain bran is limited due to the absence of a developed industry. The small amount of cotton-seed cake produced is used for export, and the amount of sesame cake produced from local oil presses is meager. Dried crop residue, mainly sorghum stalk, is the major feed source available for animal requirements. The quality of these stalks from a nutritional point of view is low.

2. Animal Disease Constraints

Animal diseases are another constraint on livestock development in Yemen. The high demand for fresh meat in Yemen has led to imports of live animals to supplement local production. In the absence of adequate quarantine control measures, live animal imports from epidemic countries have introduced several diseases to Yemen. This began during the time when animal health control services were just starting; thus, it was practically impossible to take any eradication measures due to lack of staff, facilities and supplies. Farmer attitudes towards vaccination at the beginning added another obstacle to achieving full control.

Uncontrolled livestock importation, mainly through smuggling, is continuing to exacerbate the problem. Development of a veterinary field service is going to be a long-term process; so the effect of diseases will continue for a while.

The nature and the extent of the spread of various diseases and internal parasites are not yet determined.

3. Animal Productivity Constraints

The local animals' productivity is generally low due to long-term natural selection, in which the animals' ability to survive under harsh conditions was the determining factor. To what degree the local animals will respond to an improved environment is still debatable. Some progress in improving indigenous sheep performance under improved management and feeding practices has been achieved. Unfortunately, whether the cost of such improvement is economical or not is yet to be determined.

Other results indicate that local sheep respond to improved feeding by increasing fat deposit on the tail. Although sheep and goats generally use the same feed resources, goats have greater body weight, which indicates that local goats have a better conversion rate than sheep.

The growth rate of sheep is very low. The available

results indicate that under traditional conditions the growth rate from birth to six months ranges from 66 grams to 80 grams per day.[2] On the other hand, local breeds are well adapted to adverse and harsh environments.

4.   Prevailing Animal Husbandry and Management Practice Constraints.

Yemeni farmers have developed certain husbandry and management practices which are suited to this environment and match their modest requirements for animal rearing. However, current practices concerning animal housing, feeding, selection and breeding will need to change in order to expand livestock production. Convincing any farmer to change his practices can be very easy, if the benefits can be demonstrated. Unfortunately, most of these changes have long-term gestation and the benefit cannot be immediately demonstrated. Hand feeding of cattle, for example, is not practicable in a situation where more than one cow has to be fed or in case of meeting the feeding requirements of high-demanding, productive, imported cows.

5.   Institutional Constraints

Livestock development in Yemen requires intensive efforts in many directions. This will require strong institutions with a wide range of staffing to monitor and facilitate such development. The present shortage of technical staff at all levels means building such institutions will take a long time.

An animal resource directorate should have four sections: animal health, animal production, range and forage, and wild animals and game. Each of these departments should be divided into units. As an example, animal production should include dairy, poultry, hides and skins, and extension units. Through lack of staff, the Director of Animal Resources is currently taking charge of all of these departments, and the department functions are carried out by donor projects, not department staff.

FFYP staff requirements in the livestock field and the actual numebers are shown in Table VIII-2.

TABLE VIII-2

NUMBER OF NEEDED AND AVAILABLE TECHNICAL STAFF

IN LIVESTOCK SUB-SECTOR DURING FFYP[3]

	Vet.	Agr. Eng.	Vet. Asst.	Vet. Att.
Requested	30	21	60	180
Available	4	15	5	3
Shortage	26	6	55	177

Under the pressure of the demand for livestock products and the complexity of development of the traditional livestock sub-sector, the general policy is directed towards short-term rather than long-term measures. The general approach is direct government involvement in production which, given the shortage of resources available, is the most expensive and least effective way to go about raising production.

A livestock research institution to provide a basis for extension does not exist. The same applies to extension. A veterinary field service covering the whole country is yet to be developed. Government revenues should be employed in building up institutions which, in turn, can assist thousands of farmers to raise the productivity of their livestock.

D.   Constraints to Poultry Development

1.   Feed Constraint

Lack of a local grain surplus at a reasonable price and insufficient agricultural by-products to suppport local poultry feed manufacturing ensures that most of the feed used will be imported. Feed importation is therefore a permanent feature of the poultry industry for the foreseeable future.

2.   Institutional Constraint

The poultry industry is growing fast in Yemen. This expansion is not coupled with the growth of support institutions and many management mistakes already have been made in every stage of poultry production, investment and management. The only government support available is a small section at the central veterinary lab headed by the only Yemeni poultry disease specialist. She, in effect, is taking care of all extension and disease control throughout the country.

E. Approaches to Overcoming Livestock Development Constraints

1. Approaches to Overcoming Forage Constraints

The most promising source for increasing forage production in Yemen is the natural range, which extends over some 18 million ha. of arid and semi-arid rangeland. It is recognized that the range situation in general has deteriorated alarmingly.

Improving current rangeland productivity is no doubt very complicated and a long-term issue. Much information is needed regarding vegetation and soils by areas. The most suitable technological approaches to prevailing traditional practices and the complicated land tenure system must be determined. Although different approaches have been tested in other places in the world with different degrees of success and failure, it will still be difficult to choose the most appropriate approaches without first testing for adaptability to Yemen. Intensive applied research regarding the Savory grazing method, phosphate applications, rotational and deferred grazing systems, etc., is greatly needed to determine the most economically and socially feasible route. Adapting rather than changing the prevailing system of grazing rights must be the determining policy.

Establishment of a range unit within the MAF to handle this activity is essential. As the problems of range improvement are always associated with soils, watershed management and forestry, it is highly recommended that the whole issue be considered as a part of natural resource conservation. This necessitates that the range department be a division within the Natural Resources Directorate, which should also include soil conservation, watershed development and the forestry division. Having the range division under such a structure will be more appropriate than having the unit remain with the Animal Resources Directorate.

Range improvement will be a long-term process. In addition, therefore, short-term and medium-term approaches such as the following have to be tested:

a. The possibility of using long-term fallow land for combined forage production and soil fertility enhancement;

b. Improving straw quality through mechanical methods;

c. Introduction of non-protein supplement;

d. Introduction of high yielding forage varieties with minimum requirements for water to complement sorghum and alfalfa.

2.   Overcoming Animal Disease Constraints

In general, the present effort toward establishing an animal disease control service in Yemen is satisfactory. Improving this service to the level that is capable of coping with the huge task will require more resources. The following recommendations need to be considered.

a.   Livestock importation must be strictly controlled and supervised. The animal disease control service must have authority and capability to execute quarantine regulations and rules.

b.   It will be necessary to establish new quarantines in addition to the existing ones to ensure that all the introduced animals undergo needed inspection.

c.   The rate of expansion of field service stations must be accelerated to make the rules actually effective.   .

d.   Local training of Yemenis will have to be stepped up. Coordination and clear linkages with other health units in the rural develoment projects need to be established.

e.   A general disease survey is needed in each region, followed by eradication programs.

f.   Regular internal and external parasite control measures need to be introduced.

3.   Overcoming Animal Productivity Constraints

Both cross-breeding and introduction of other exotic breeds will be necessary measures in the future. Although the local breeds are considered as poor productive animals, they have other desirable characteristics, such as high resistance to diseases and the ability to reproduce themselves under harsh conditions.

Basically, before any introduction or cross-breeding measures are undertaken, some solid information on local breeds' performance under the improved conditions has to be gathered and analyzed, especially for economic feasibility. Such investigation can be conducted in parallel with testing the performance of different exotic breeds under a reasonably improved local environment, in addition to cross-breeding experiments.

Effort should be concentrated on small ruminants (sheep and goats) rather than cattle. It is abundantly clear that small ruminants are the most suitable type of livestock in Yemen's environment: Thus it is difficult to justify on technical or economic grounds the current expenditure of resources on cattle projects.

4. Overcoming Animal Husbandry and Management Production Constraints

Upgrading farmers' animal husbandry skills through extension which will have short-term effects, such as improving animal feeding practices through introduction of mineral and protein supplements, regular vaccination campaigns, internal parasite control, and introducing hand operated straw choppers.

Mechanisms for collecting data concerning traditional production cost and profitabliliy pertaining to small livestock enterprises will have to be established. From this data, villagers can be given appropriate assistance in improving the productivity of their animals.

With sound data, upgrading of other husbandry aspects can be started. This will include culling and selection, housing, drylot feeding, cross-breeding and introduction of exotic breeds.

Generally, upgrading must start with improving what is available in the system rather than introducing a new system.

5. Overcoming Institutional Constraints

Strengthening the Animal Resources Directorate's capability is a vital issue to livestock development in the YAR. The Directorate's research and extension capacities deserve high priorities. The present governmental poultry, dairy and livestock finishing operations can be a good basis for data collection, research and extension. Their contributions to livestock development through these activities will be greater than what they can provide as commercial enterprises. Issues, priorities and realistic targets have to be established to facilitate rational use of the limited available staff and facilities.

Directorate capability for providing needed services to

both traditional and modern livestock producers in the form of animal health services and the supplying of needed inputs has to be built up. Major emphasis and efforts should be directed toward facilitating and encouraging farm level production rather than involvement in direct government production projects.

The Directorate's functional presence in potential production regions has to be developed.

6. Approches to Overcoming Poultry Constraints

The poultry industry is going to require a strong poultry service to facilitate and encourage industry development.

The service should have a high capability to deal with disease problems from diagnostic, preventative and curative aspects. Other functions would be in facilitating and monitoring the flow of needed inputs, advising in promotion of sound technological approaches, training of producers, and controlling the quality of imported and locally produced inputs. The poultry service would also be involved in testing and encouraging local poultry feed production.

The existing facilities provide a good basis for rendering such services.

F. Strategic Considerations

There is a great need to develop livestock in Yemen to meet the increasing demand for animal protein. The potential for such development exists and the ongoing efforts need to be complemented. Based on these facts, the following priorities are suggested:

1.   Institutional focus.

Strengthening the Animal Resources Directorate and establishing adequate units to deal with animal production and health constraints are essential requirements. Research and extension capability are currently the weakest components.

2.   Range and Forage Production.

The ongoing efforts cannot cope with the complexity of the problem. The issue is connected with the whole natural resources conservation problem which, in fact, is the least addressed but the most elemental issue facing Yemen.

3.   Small Ruminants

Sheep and goats have the major potential for supplying additional meat and milk. Efforts toward improving their productivity should be given higher priority. Resources currently spent on government dairy production projects would have a far greater impact if deployed for small ruminant improvement projects.

NOTES

[1]   Yemen Araba Republic.   Statistical Year Book,
CPO, Sanaa, 1981

[2]   MOD.   Project Report 16-YAR-d-29/Rep-16/77.

[3]   SFYP proposed draft.

IX. WATER RESOURCES AND IRRIGATION MANAGEMENT

This section deals with water as a resource for
agricultural development through irrigation. The setting
under which development is occurring will be described
initially, followed by specific development issues in the
water sector.

A.   Setting for Irrigation Development

The MAF was one of the first ministries to be created
in the YARG, along with the Ministry of Public Works. Each
of these ministries included a department of irrigation,
which led to confusion regarding their respective roles. In
1973 the MAF was assigned sole responsibility for
irrigation. During this same year, the TDA was created with
the Minister of Agriculture as chairman of the board and
this authority was responsible for development in the Tihama
region. In 1976 SURDU was established to implement an
IBRD/FAO-supported integrated rural development project
covering the southern provinces of Ibb and Taiz. For the
eastern valleys and the Central and Northern Highlands, the
GDI is responsible for irrigation development. There are
also semi-autonomous agencies responsible for irrigation
development in their specified geographic areas. A brief
discussion of these agencies follows:

1.   **The General Directorate of Irrigation (GDI)**

The GDI was the first governmental institution to be given full responsibility for developing and managing YARG's water resources.   Because of inadequate resources of both manpower and funds, the GDI has confined its activities to developmental and investigative work on watersheds of the western slopes and Central Highlands.   Specifically, their activities are confined to:

a.   Supervising and managing the development of the Marib Dam project (supported by the Abu Dhabi Fund);

b.   Supervising the investigative activities of Wadi Jawf and its tributaries (under contract with Agrar-und Hydrotechnik GMBH, Federal Republic of Germany);

c.   Design and construction of small dams in the Northern and Central Highlands;

d.   Supervising the investigation of the Sanaa groundwater basin (supported by the USSR);

e.   Maintaining agricultural terraces;

f.   Groundwater development.

The funds for support of the GDI come principally from the YARG budget and these totaled YR 22 million in 1982. Activities in terrace maintenance and small diversion dam construction are financed totally through the MAF.   Eight small dams have been repaired and three new ones have been constructed to date.   Terrace maintenance has been limited to stabilizing terraces near stream channels.

The GDI has expatriate engineers as principal advisor and assistant engineer. Two other expatriate civil engineers also work in the department. There are no Yemeni engineers within the GDI.

2. Tihama Development Authority

This authority was created by Law No. 2 and amended by Law No. 8, 1973. The TDA has been given responsibility by the MAF for developing and managing water resources within the geographical areas of the Tihama or coastal region. Its legal powers include:

a. To own the _wadi_ beds within defined limits;

b. To demolish any existing works or to construct any new works within these limits;

c. To regulate and control the distribution and use of all surface water;

d. To regulate the development of groundwater;

e. To operate wells and to sell water to others at rates set by TDA.

The TDA is supervising five major _wadi_ projects. The projects are in various stages of planning, investigation, construction or completion. Details of plans for these projects can be found in various feasibility studies, all of which have been reviewed by Merabet.[1]

3. Southern Uplands Rural Development Unit

Established in 1976, SURDU operates as a semi-autonomous unit under the MAF, but as yet it is not an authority. SURDU has responsibilities for MAF water resource activities and acts through the MAF province offices at Ibb and Taiz. SURDU is involved in the design and construction of village water supply facilities. It also handled irrigation development for the IBRD/FAO project in this geographical area, as well as providing technical assistance to projects of the LDA.

B.   Other YARG Agencies

There are a number of other YARG agencies that are also involved in irrigation development as mentioned below.

1.   Yemen Oil and Mineral Corporation

YOMINCO has a Department of Hydrology which collects hydrologic data pertaining to surface and groundwater supplies and carries out specific studies in water-related fields. This department was created on recommendation by a USAID water survey team.

2.   Civil Aviation and Meteorological Authority

This authority was given the responsibility in 1978 to collect, analyze and distribute meteorological data for the entire country. It would be of great value to irrigation planning if this authority's functions were also to include collection and analysis of agrometeorological data.

3.   National Water and Sewage Authority

This authority was established in 1973 to locate,

exploit and distribute water for domestic, commercial and industrial uses in urban areas. The NWSA is at present supervising the design and construction of water and sewage systems for the five major towns of Sanaa, Hodeidah, Taiz, Ibb and Dhamar. Seven international companies are involved in the construction. The NWSA could play an important role in the use of sewage effluent for irrigation.

4.   Confederation of the Yemeni Development Associations

During the period from 1968 to 1975, extreme shortages in domestic water supply were a major element in the formation of LDA. In June 1973 a group of LDA held a conference and created CYDA as an umbrella organization with links to the government and some foreign donors. CYDA channels the foreign donor funds to the LDA. CYDA is not a governmental agency, but rather a paragovernmental body. It operates as a federation of LDA presided over by the President of the YAR. Some LDA have become involved in small-scale irrigation projects, in addition to domestic water supply, roads, schools, etc.

c.   Resource Assessment for Irrigation

Rainfall is the basic water resource in the YAR, as there are no lakes or perennial rivers in the country. In the Tihama, annual rainfall is between zero and 150 mm., often below the minimal amount needed for rainfed agriculture. In the lower western escarpment from 500-1,400

m. elevation, rainfall is between 200-4000 mm. per year, while in the high western mountains up to 1,800 mm. falls annually. The highest and most consistent rainfall occurs in the Southern Highlands near Ibb. There is little rainfall in the eastern parts of the YAR, which borders the famous Empty Quarter desert of the peninsula. Even though some data have been collected at recently installed rain gauge stations, accurate and long-term data on Yemeni rainfall patterns are lacking.

During recent geologic times, the soil and rock strata have accumulated water from rainfall and runoff. This groundwater, which now comprises a substantial portion of the YAR's water exploitation, is a resource that urgently needs to be assessed, as its depletion is a major concern for the YARG. Recent studies have shown that the water table in the Sanaa basin is being depleted at the rate of two meters per year.[2]

Runoff from most of the <u>wadis</u> occurs as spate flow, as described in a summary by the CID Water Policy Initiatives report:

> The Western Escarpment has seven major wadis. They all drain westward to the Tihama. For most of the year only small streamlets run into the wadi through April and again from July to September, several heavy floods normally occur along the whole length of the wadi sources. The farmers build earthen barages in the middle of the wadi beds to divert the flood waters into cultivated lands, irrigated by the ancient practice of spate

irrigation. If the rainfall is unusually heavy
within the whole catchment area, the floods may be
large enough to reach the coast of the Red Sea;
but this occurrence is exceptional.

The gradients of the wadis of the Eastern
Escarpment are smaller and the precipitation in
the inter-regions of the country is less intensive
and does not occur with the same seasonal regu-
larity as on the rain exposed Western Escarpment.
But the catchment areas are larger and thus the
floods may cause inundation of large areas for
long periods. In ancient times, earthen dams at
Marib and Jawf made possible cultivation of large
areas in these regions. Since the Sixth Century
A.D. the dams have been broken and the population
of this area has diminished considerably.

In the Central Highlands, drainage is not
always connected with the large wadi systems. The
rainfall is often retained on cultivated fields
and any surplus waters may remain trapped in
interior basins. But if the rainfalls are heavy,
the floods from the highland plans will discharge
in larger wadi systems.

The water supply is a major constraint on
agricultural production. Thus the knowledge of
the proportion of rainfall which can be made
available for crop growth is of great importance.
While no accurate measurements exist, a Swiss
report for the Dhamar Plain indicates approximately 70 percent of the rain which falls on
uncultivated land becomes runoff, of which one-
third enters into the streanflow and two-thirds
are diverted onto cultivated lands.[3]

In a report prepared for the GDI in November, 1981, on

available water resources, it was estimated that about three

billion cubic meters of water are available from the western

slopes and about one billion from the eastern slopes for

irrigation. The quantity of surface and groundwater used

for irrigation on the western slopes alone is 829 million

and 206 million cubic meters, respectively. Since irrigated

areas represent a production capacity three or four times

that of rainfed areas, there is a potentially expandable area to be irrigated. Of a total of 1.5 million ha. of cultivated land in the YAR, only 250,000 are irrigated. Half of this is irrigated by spate in the coastal region and foothills.

Springs are an important source for domestic water supply and irrigation, especially in the highlands. It is estimated that a third of all households in the YAR depend on springs for potable water. Although springs are mostly dependent on rainfall patterns for recharge, spring irrigation offers the farmer a more secure water supply than spate irrigation in the coastal region.[4] In most cases the spring flow is diverted into reservoirs, some of which are lined with a natural cement or concrete. Spring flow is a shared resource in Islamic water law and allocation is according to a rotating cycle of turns. Irrigated terrace farming produces a wide variety of crops, including sorghum, coffee, qat, tomatoes, vegetable and fruit trees.

D.   Present and Future Plans

Irrigation development plans focus largely on the development of water supply for irrigation rather than the development of irrigation systems per se. The development of irrigation water supply focuses on diversion of spate flows, exploitation of perennial flows and groundwater wells.

Table IX-1 shows the ongoing and proposed projects for development of irrigation water, other related activities and the proposed SFYP funding level as a percentage of the total. The budget for each individual project activity is made up from anticipated donor and YARG funds. These two portions of total project support are expressed as a percentage of the total YARG and donor support, respectively. Donors that have expressed an interest or made a firm commitment are also listed.

The table serves only to identify MAF priorities in their development of projects. Of course, donor participation and interest in developing certain projects in the YAR tends to bias MAF priorities. For example, the Abu Dhabi Fund is interested only in the reconstruction of the Marib dam, because of historical links with ancient Yemeni civilization. The Marib project probably will never become economically viable, but it will consume 28% of the total budget allocation for water resources in the next five years to only serve a few thousand farmers at the most. Most of the investment in water resources is for wadi development in the Tihama. Development of Wadi Mawr will take about a third of the money allotted for water resources in the SFYP.

The ongoing public sector development projects and proposed new projects shown in Table IX-1 are largely for

TABLE IX-1

PRESENT AND PROPOSED IRRIGATION WATER DEVELOPMENT PROJECTS

THE MAF SFYP PLAN*

	YARG Support	Foreign Donors		Total Irrigation Investment over next 5 years
Ongoing Projects	%	%		%
Tihama Projects				
Wadi Zabid	1.65	0.66	None**	0.95
Wadi Rima	27.17	12.91	WB-Kuwait Fund	17.06
Wadi Mawr	40.21	29.67	WB, Kuwait IFAD, EEC German	32.74
Wadi Siham	0.36	0.22	None	0.26
Other Projects				
Wadi Jawf Develop.	7.74	8.37	None	8.19
Small Weir Construction	3.35	5.51	UNDP/FAO	4.89
Groundwater Develop.	0.65	0.89	None	0.82
Proposed New Projects				
Marib Dam	9.68	35.78	Abu Dhabi (UAE)	28.18
Study of Northern Wadis	0.97	0.40	Japanese	0.56
Water Assessment Projects				
Agromet Stations	0.52	0	None	0.15
Maintenance of Terraces	1.55	0.64	None	0.90
Survey of Water Resources	0.97	1.19	None	1.13
Application of Modern Irrigation Tech.	0.52	0.21	UNDP	0.13
Study of Sewage Water for Irrigation		0.36	None	0.26
Study and Development of Sanaa Basin	4.65	3.18	USSR	3.61
TOTALS	100.00	100.00		100.00

---

* Statistics from the General Directorate of Statistics and Planning Department, MAF.

** Even though no donor has been identified, expected funds have been estimated.

development of spate and perennial flows. The development of groundwater is largely a private sector activity. In 1981, the MAF reported that 72,000 ha. of land were irrigated by pumpwells. By the end of the SFYP, 120,000 ha. are expected to be irrigated from wells. However, despite fears of falling water tables in important regions of the YAR, only .82% of the SFYP budget for public sector irrigation development is for groundwater development, largely well constuction. Apparently there are no plans for development of spring water. Such an activity would be more appropriate under LDA auspices.

E.   Development Issues and Analysis

1.   Approach of Wadi Development Using Spate and Perennial Flows

Table IX-1 shows that a high percentage (79%) of the GDI five-year budget is going into the construction of hydraulic structures and associated canals and roads on coastal wadis to increase supplies or irrigation water. While it is proper to develop associated infrastructure of the wadis, there appears to be insufficient attention given to resources and manpower needed over the next five years for the operation and maintenance of complete projects. In addition, little or no attention is directed towards the management of water after it leaves the main diversion canals. Efficient water usage is a major constraint to the proper management of these diverted flows and their subsequent distribution and application.

The IBRD Agricultural Sector Study[5] concludes that the YARG should proceed with construction projects already initiated, but future attention should be focused on developing distribution and utilization systems rather than undertaking new construction projects. Greater production can be achieved on fewer systems by more efficient management of water, crops and oils where control of spate and perennial flows has been obtained, as opposed to more projects that are inefficiently operated or maintained. The issue of water rights, or the equitable distribution of water for proposed wadi development, must be addressed by the government if efficient irrigation systems are to be developed. Procedures and methods for working out formal agreements with landowners regarding water shares before initiation of construction would be an important part of a strategy for achieving efficient irrigation.

As noted in Table IX-1, it is anticipated that UNDP/FAO will assist the MAF with the development of small dams and weirs. There are several anticipated sites where the MAF would like to develop a storage reservoir for irrigation development and groundwater recharge. FAO is willing to develop the design, but does not have funds for capital construction. Development of a model system is appropriate but, distribution and on-farm water management, as well as agreement on water rights, must equally be part of any system. The investment for such a reservoir and irrigation system is high, but so are the returns from the increased agricultural production downstream.

2.   Low Irrigation Efficiency

In a country that is defined as water deficient, efficiency of water use should have the highest priority. Improper irrigation methods contribute to wasted water that could be used to expand the total irrigated area. Low irrigation efficiencies also depress crop yields. These low yields are usually the result of improper irrigation frequency, loss of nitrogen and other nutrients and poor aeration in the root zone.

Preliminary research investigation by the CARS on irrigation practices for grapes near Sanaa in the Central Highlands showed that farmers were applying six times more water than needed (450 cm/year) to produce the same grape crop. If one assumes that this exorbitant use of water occurs in all grape cultivations and if 300 cm. of water could be saved per year over the total grape area of 12,000 hectares, a total annual savings of $360,000m^3$ of water would be achieved. The simple practice of furrowing alone would reduce the width of the soil surface receiving irrigation water and produce water savings of 50%. Since the water table is deep in the Central Highlands and salinity is not a problem, high irrigation efficiencies (80%) could be achieved through proper on-farm water management using well established techniques and equipment. If, for the sake of illustration, the average well in the Sanaa basin produces six liters/second, the water saved is equal to the yield of about 1,929 wells pumping continuously throughout the year.

Obviously, one cannot extrapolate this low irrigation efficiency over the entire area cultivated in grapes, since many farmers pruchase well water from neighbors who have producing wells. Purchased water will obviously be used more efficiently than "free" water from a wadi. Nonetheless, the above example illustrates a very important issue that the government must face. Once again, the payoff from the investment of supplying water through diversion dams and/or wells comes from proper management of this water resource by the crisumer. The payoff in construction projects lies in what can te produced by the water resource after it is brought under control.

3. Inadequate Agrometerological Data and Recording Stations

It is not possible to manage water resources, soils and crops without a knowledge of the magnitude of the resources and the climatic factors which provide the basis for deci-

sion making. It is difficult to determine water requirements for crops or to make proper crop selections where only
scattered climatological data are available. The proper
design of irrigation systems depends upon adequate climatological data on the area under consideration. Due to the
diverse climates that exist in the four or five regions of
the country and the diversity of climate within regions,
more agrometeorological stations are needed. According to
Table IX-1, less than .15% of the MAF five-year budget is
allocated to establish such stations and for personnel to be
trained in disciplined, systematic data collection.

4.   Inadequate Water Policy and Excessive Groundwater With-
      drawals

      The "Water Policy Initiatives for Yemen" report by
Bernhardt, et al. in 1980 is still a useful document in
this context. The report's rationale for the establishment
of national policies is that:

> The current rapid rate of economic development and
> raising economic expectations of the people
> coupled with studies and proposals for water pro-
> jects give emphasis to this need. What is needed
> is a policy in which the national government ful-
> fills its leadership role in setting direction and
> taking initiatives for the common good, but which,
> at the same time, can promote wisdom in water use
> at the local level and is flexible enough to deal
> with a range of local conditions.[6]

The management of the groundwater resource through the
proposed National Groundwater Act should be an urgent high-

priority governmental concern. However, the government is indecisive on the issue of establishing laws and policies regarding exploitation of groundwater resources. Wells are being drilled presently at the rate of about 1,500 per year; data on the distribution and location of these wells are not available, but apparently most of the drilling is taking place in the Southern Highlands. Furthermore, it is estimated that 80-90% of the wells are used for qat production; or, at least a portion of each well flow is used for qat, which provides the cash flow to underwrite the investment costs of well installation. Information is lacking regarding the number of other crops irrigated from wells primarily for qat. Qat is obviously financing most of Yemen's groundwater development, but depletion of groundwater resources for irrigation of this nonfood crop may jeopardize national interests. Accurate water-use data on qat irrigation is a crucial need at this time.

It should also be emphasized here that commercial irrigation of crops by well water is a totally new concept in the YAR. In light of probable groundwater depletion, an initial requirement for government involvement is developing the efficient use of well water through demonstration and extension work. Excessive irrigation from surface flows or wells does not return to the groundwater for immediate reuse. It is true that some of the excess will percolate into the groundwater aquifer for use at some future time. However, soil profiles with deep water tables, more than 50 meters, and varying degrees of soil stratification may require many years before surface applications will reach the water table. If the groundwater table is being lowered at a greater rate than the downward flow of water, this excess water will not have an immediate effect upon recharge.

5. Terrace Deterioration

The issue of terrace deterioration is of major importance in the YAR, but the MAF is placing only 0.9% of its five-year budget into maintenance of terraces. The consequences of significant terrace deterioration, due to labor shortages for traditional agricultural work and the marginality of rainfed agriculture, can be the collapse of an entire local terrace system in a domino effect. A cursory analysis suggests that a system may be drastically affected by erosion of terraces located at critical positions on the slope. There is a need for accurate data on the rate and scope of terrace deterioration in the YAR. While YARG should not be responsible for individual terrace repair or maintenance, it should provide advice and technological expertise to help farmers tackle their terrace problems.

6. Use of Sewage Effluent in Irrigation

USAID has financed a CID study team to investigate this issue and the report is now available.

F.   Strategic Consideration

Water management in the YAR needs high priority in the government's overall development strategy. Successful management of water resources will ensure increased agricultural production. The greatest impact upon water management can be made through improved on-farm management. Building the ministry's capabilities in on-farm water management will permit the government to proceed with an integrated approach to irrigation development. Extension of water management concepts to farmers for both surface and groundwater supplies should be the key strategy. Once the government has the capacity to handle such a program, this extension process must be accomplished through demonstration programs.

On-farm water management demonstration should be programmed into every <u>wadi</u> development project in the Tihama as well as in areas where pumpwell development is occurring. Pumpowners and large, influential farmers should be targeted, since their practices influence smaller farmers, especially in the control and distributon of water along a <u>wadi</u>. It is expected that the process of change to more efficient allocation and management may be slow. While the Yemeni farmer is usually quick to accept and implement economically beneficial innovations, the social, legal and technical issues are complex and must be approached with caution.

1. Technical Assistance.

At present there are no on-farm water management engineers in the YAR, either expatriate or Yemeni nationals. The need for resident expatriate technicians with small-farm, arid-area qualifications is acute. Such a resident specialist in the GDI could facilitate technology transfer and expand the ministry's capabilities in this area.

2. Training

There is an immediate and urgent need for training Yemeni agricultural engineers to work in the MAF. These engineers need training in the soil and water aspects of agricultural engineering.

3. Extension

The extension program in the YAR must include a section dealing with on-farm water management. The training component of the implementation strategy should include short training courses in on-farm water management. No other donors have as yet addressed this type of extension activity.

4. Demonstration farms.

The importance of this type of activity has already been addressed. It would be of great value to have a prototype demonstration farm for use as a model by the MAF in wadi development strategy.

NOTES

1 Zohra Merabet, A Survey on Development and Management of Water Resources in the Yemen Arab Republic, Sanaa, May 1980.

2 This is an estimate from the MAF, corroborated by well drilling companies.

3 Charles F. Bernhardt, et al., Water Resources Development Program Framework for the Yemen Arab Republic, CID, 1980.

4 Daniel Martin Varisco, The Adaptive Dynamics of Water Allocation in al-Ahjur, Yemen Arab Republic, Ph.D. Dissertation, Univeristy of Pennsylvania, 1982.

5 IBRD, Agricultural Sector Study, 1981.

6 Charles F. Bernhardt, et al, Op. cit.

X. FISHERIES

A. Background

The fisheries sector in the YAR is quite small, with an estimated 3,000 full-time fishermen living in about 40 fishing communities. Another several hundred fishermen work in Saudi Arabia at Jizan, but they return home during the month of Ramadan. The local fleet consists of less than 1,000 vessels, which, along with beach seiners, bring in an annual catch of 12,000 tons, as estimated by FAO and the World Bank, or 17,500 tons, as estimated by the YARG.

Rapid structural changes have occurred in the fisheries sector in recent years. Migration to Saudi Arabia has improved the fishermen's lot. Vessel ownership is shifting from shore-based entrepreneurs to fishermen operating the vessels themselves. The fishermen's share of the catch has grown from one-third to one-half.

B. Fish Resources

The YAR has a coastline of approximately 600 km., with a continental shelf of 9,100 sq. km. Data are scarce, but limited exploratory work indicates that the trawlable area is more than 6,000 sq. km., of which about 550 sq. km. are considered good shrimp grounds. The potential yield of demersal fish over the trawlable area is estimated at 7,800 tons. The non-trawlable area will yield 5,000 tons for a total demersal fish resource of 12,000 to 13,000 tons. About 70% of the national catch consists of pelagic species, dominated by herring, mackeral, sardines, anchovies and tuna. Resources of these fish are estimated at 8,000 tons, twice the existing catch. Total shrimp biomass is estimated at 1,700 tons for a sustained annual yield of 850 tons. Altogether, the country's fish resource is estimated at 25,000-30,000 tons per year.

C. Fishing Methods

There are two types of fishing vessels in operation in the YAR. The sambuk is 11-15 m. long and the houri is 6-10 m. long. The sambuk is well adapted to the marine conditions prevailing in the Red Sea. These days it carries a crew of 6-8 men and is powered by a 22-33 hp. inboard diesel. The houri is a planked canoe, which today is frequently powered by a 6-10 hp. outboard motor and is operated by two men.

Boat building is done by individual boat builders, who build on order for a contractor. Fishing boats are still being built without the help of power tools or mechanical devices. The contractor purchases all materials, including the engine. For planking, Malaysian hardwood is used; for the vessel's frame, domestic wood is chosen. The methods and materials make boat construction an expensive undertaking. A fully equipped 15 m. sambuk, for example, costs over YR 130,000, while a <u>houri</u> with engine costs YR 25,000.

The main fishing techniques employed are gill netting with imported nylon nets and single hooks and lines. <u>Sambuks</u> usually carry 10-15 nets, which are manually operated. Fishermen on <u>houris</u> use hand lines with two to three baited hooks. In most villages beach seines are used during season to catch sardines and anchovies.

Fishing is done at night or early in the morning. <u>Sambuks</u> leave before sunset and return after sunrise, while the <u>houris</u> leave before dawn and return a few hours later. Fishing takes place inshore close to the landing site and around offshore islands along the northern coastline. The average annual number of fishing days is about 200 for <u>houris</u> and 225 for <u>sambuks</u>. Catch rates vary significantly, depending on the location and vessel size, but the average is estimat d at 5 tons per year for the <u>houris</u> and 49 tons per year for the <u>sambuks</u>. The best approximation for the national fleet was 972 vessels in 1979/80, comprising 815 <u>houris</u> and 157 <u>sambuks</u>. Based on the number of vessels and the catch rates, total fish landings amount to approximately 11,600 tons per year. On the basis of YR 10 per kg., the total value of the catch for fishermen is YR 110.6 million. In addition, 60 <u>sambuks</u> operate exclusively out of Jizan in Saudi Arabia catching 3-4,000 tons of fish in Yemeni waters.

Hodeidah accounts for over 40% of the national catch. Landings north of Hodeidah, where demersal fish predominate, account for a quarter of the catch, while landings south of Hodeidah, where most species are pelagic, account for a third of the catch. Nearly two-thirds of the total catch is mackeral.

D. Marketing

Hodeidah and nine other landing sites account for all the marketed fish. Another 30 villages fish for local consumption only. Fish are brought to the auction site near the landing beach. Here they are thrown onto the sand, without protection from the sun, for inspection by buyers. Fish are sold by bundles, each with similar-sized fish of the same species. Sales are for cash to the highest bidder. In the villages the auctioneers charge 5%, but their fee is 10% in Hodeidah. Buyers are usually dealers, who bring their own ice and distribute fish throughout the Tihama and to major urban centers in the highlands. The auctioneers maintain records of the kinds of fish, units or bundles, prices and names of the fishermen.

Fish handling throughout the YAR, except at Hodeidah and Taiz, is deplorable. Despite abundance of ice, fishermen do not use it on board the boats. Auction sites at landings have no cover, so even the freshest fish face rapid deterioration. These sites are often sand patches and have no water for cleaning. Conditions for the retail sale of fish are below acceptable international standards, with fish exposed to heat, dust and flies. In these circumstances, fish loses much of its nutritive value by the time it reaches the inland markets.

E. Prices and Incomes

The average price of fish at landing sites is about YR 10 per kg. today, up from YR 6 per kg. in 1980. Retail prices are at least YR 30 per kg. Over the past few years, fish prices have increased at twice the rate of the consumer price index. Prices have been drawn up by growing income levels and the very high price of fresh meat, particularly mutton, veal and beef. In 1980 fish sold for about the same price as imported broiler chickens, at about YR 15, but now fish has risen in value to equal that of local baladi chickens.

A major factor contributing to the relative increase in fish prices is the vastly improved distribution system. Although fishermen and retailers can do much to improve the way they handle fish, the distributors do a reasonably good job. Given the large demand and shortage of supply, nearly all fish are sold to the final consumer in two days. At the landing sites, sales are quick and distributors preserve the fish in ice. More efficient distribution of fish in recent years has increased availability in the major highland towns. The improved product has been well received by consumers, whose only alternative is imported, processed fish. Imports of processed fish, mostly canned, in 1979, cost YR 28 million.

Fish prices vary considerably according to species, location and daily volume of catch. In 1980 the short-term supply/price relationship in Hodeidah indicated variations between 80% and 120%. Such daily fluctuation can be attributed to lack of storage capacity, which has been ameliorated by the improved efficiency of the distribution system. This improvement has also reduced the differential in prices between the coast and inland centers to more acceptable levels.

Annual per capita fresh fish consumption is estimated at 2 kg., ranging from 60 kg. in the fishing villages to almost zero in inland mountain villages. The most noticeable growth in consumption is in the main urban centers.

Annual income for fishermen in 1980 was estimated at YR 11,000, amounting to a per capita income of $430 for the fishing community. The actual level of income depends on various factors, the most important being productivity. Sambuk fishermen have twice the productivity of houri fishermen--nine tons per year compared with four tons per year. In 1980 a fisherman operating a motorized sambuk earned an annual income averaging YR 16,100, while the operator of a _houri_ only earned YR 3,300. These estimates can probably be raised by 60% to account for recent rises in fish prices.

F. Governmental Involvement

Governmental involvement in fisheries did not really start until 1979, with the establishment of the Department of Fisheries (DOF), within the MAF. In 1980 the government established the General Corporation for the Development of Fish Resources (GCDFR), a parastatal organization reporting to the Minister of Fisheries. The DOF is to formulate policy guidelines for the sector, while the GCDFR is the executing agency for the MAF. During the FFYP, an ambitious YR 94.4 million development plan was drawn up for six projects, but only YR 9 million was actually spent.

While there has been assistance from the USSR, FAO and DANIDA, the most important factor in fisheries development has been the World Bank/IDA project of YR 136 million. Administered by the GCDFR, this project is to improve artisanal fisheries through investment in fishing ports, improved distribution and marketing, credit for equipment purchase, roads, technical assistance and training. If completed according to plan, the project will have fully integrated the artisanal fishermen into the economy and installed an infrastructure for self-sustained growth in production.

G. Strategic Considerations

The major issue with respect to fisheries is the role of GCDFR in developing the fisheries industry. The original intent was that it would implement the World Bank project to help improve the incomes of fishermen. In practice, the GCDFR is building its own fishing fleet and onshore facilities, using funds which should be spent for improving existing fishing communities. It has purchased boats and staffed them with GCDFR employees, who receive YR 3,000 per month. Although it has not fully implemented ongoing projects in the two years since its inception, the GCDFR has plans to expand into shrimp processing, fish meal manufacture and aquaculture. Unfortunately, the shrimp processing plant would compete with that already planned under the World Bank's project for artisanal fishermen, the fish meal plant has no economic or resource basis, and aquaculture is just not viable in Yemen under present conditions. The GCDFR should focus on increasing fish production from existing resources of fishermen, rather than competing as a parastatal operation.

XI. FORESTRY

A. Background

In ancient times Yemen contained extensive forests.
Increasing aridity brought about by a combination of
changing global climatic conditions, ever-increasing tree
cutting for fuel and timber and continual heavy browsing by
goats led to a downward spiral of deforestation. Today,
there are no continuous forests, and the cumulative effect
of forest cover depletion, soil erosion, runoff and range
deterioration is obvious. In all, the total area of the YAR
under woodland and shrub is estimated to be 1,600,000 ha.

In the Tihama, a thin strip of mangrove extends along
the coast from Hodeidah to the Saudi Arabian border.
Uncultivated areas have sparse vegetation suited to growth
under arid conditions. In the wadis and along the
foothills is a savannah cover, with acacias dominating. In
the wadi openings and flood plains, belts of tamarix and
Ficus occur, with date palms. In the midlands and
highlands are the best forest conditions, because rainfall
is higher and morning fogs frequent. Since this area is
also the most suitable for agriculture, it is intensively
terraced, confining the natural vegetation to the margins.
The dominant tree species are acacias and Euphorbiacea.
Other tree varieties include Cordia abyssinica,

junipers, christ-thorns, _Balanites aegyptiaca_, carob, tamarind, _Salvadora persica_, and _Brugieriae_. Of the recently imported trees, _Eucalyptus_ is the most common, particularly _E. camaludensis_ and _E. globulus_. Other imported species are cypress, aleppo pines, _Casuarina_, _Cassia_ and _Solonacius rustica_. Various species have their particular uses, altogether providing a whole range of benefits: fuelwood, lumber, fruits, spices, fodder, medicines, honey and gums.

B. Usage

The desirable lumber trees are the christ-thorns, junipers, tamarix, and _Cordia abyssinica_. The major usage, though, is fuelwood, followed by forage. Fuelwood consumption is estimated at about a cubic meter per capita, or 750 kg. per person per year. In the highlands, fuelwood from local sources, the Tihama, and even Saudi Arabia is sold in variously-sized bundles. A pickup load, approximately one cubic meter, sells for YR 500-1500, depending on the locality's proximity to the stands of trees.

Trees often have individual ownership, though ownership is more communal on the range. One half of the families surveyed in the Ibb and Taiz areas[1] obtained at least a quarter of their fuelwood from their own farms or homestead lots, while another quarter came from communal lands. A

-205-

quarter to a third had been purchased. Wood collection takes up a considerable amount of womanpower, an average of five hours per day yielding 10-25 kg.[2] The amount of fuelwood required by a family of five to cook just the main meal of the day was estimated at 7 kg. Since almost a third of this fuel consists of live branches, the survivability of the existing "public" trees is in doubt.

Prices of fuelwood are extremely high, thanks to rising income as well as diminishing supply. In the Ibb and Taiz survey, the following prices of fuelwood and alternative fuels prevailed in early 1982:

Fuel	Price YR/kg.
Fuelwood	1.1
Charcoal	2.4
Crop Residue	0.7
Kerosene (liter)	2.3
Butane	3.5

In terms of net energy yield, fuelwood is about the most expensive fuel in use. The traditional Yemeni stove (tannur) is fairly efficient, with its earthen construction and controlled air flow. In fact, stove types found in the Tihama are as efficient as any wood-burning cooker constructed in the third world. Still, its efficiency of combustion overall is low, probably about 15-20%. By comparison, a butane burner is 90% efficient and a kilo of butane has three times the calories as a kilo of wood. At current prices, butane cooking is half the cost of wood burning. Policy options thus are straightforward: heavily promote butane and/or step up imports of cheaper firewood, preferably via large-scale purchase of timber sawmill wastes and wood chips from wood-surplus countries. Another alternative is to import charcoal substitutes developed from coal, as done in Korea, after testing their acceptability.

The high price of fuelwood is a heavy drain on family income. The Ibb and Taiz survey estimated that fuelwood purchases cost the average family YR 5,000 per year, or 20-25% of the annual family income. In addition, annual family expenditure on lumber and poles reached YR 1,200-1,590, bringing total expenditure on fuelwood and wood products to 25-32% of family income. Combined with kerosene and butane, the survey would indicate that total fuel and timber expenditure probab'y equals that on food or gat. In this context, an energy sector study warrants immediate and highest government priority.

C.   Government Activity

The YARG has formulated a policy and established an embryonic Directorate, with a Yemeni agricultural graduate as director, plus two technicians. The policy document presents some 14 broad objectives including the promotion of land use according to land capability classification, protection of existing forest, production of tree seedlings, afforestation wherever feasible in the country, production of fuelwood, timber and fodder on a sustained yield basis, creation of recreational areas and national parks, protection of irrigation dams and agricultural lands, and creating a forest consciousness on the part of the public. This comprehensive policy is considered more than adequate for the MAF's proposed SFYP on forestry.

A draft Forestry Law has now been approved by the cabinet and awaits enactment by the National Assembly. The draft document contains eleven chapters and is fairly comprehensive and rigid in some respects. The law would provide for forest protection, investigation and confiscation of illegally acquired forest products, infringement penalties, forest utilization and management, establishment of protected areas, distribution of revenues from government forests, local rights and establishment of an afforestation fund financed by a tax on imported timber. Enforcement of the law in its present form and under present circumstances in the YAR would require a level of government policing in economic matters that is beyond current capabilitiy.

The Directorate staff is being built up with seven Yemenis undergoing university education and 32 others attending lower-level training at the Lattakia Forest Institute in

Syria. The Directorate's main responsiblity is the operation of four nurseries in Sanaa, Taiz, Ibb and Hodeidah that during the FFYP produced a million seedlings for free distribution to municipalities, LDA and individuals. In the current plan period, the target is 10 million seedlings. This will hardly make a dent on demand, which the Sanaa University survey estimated at 21.2 million seedlings for the Ibb and Taiz regions alone. One way to increase the supply of seedlings is for the MAF to gradually stop free issue to individuals and start selling seedlings at full cost. This would establish a commercial market for seedlings, which could draw in the nation's farmers to both produce and sell seedlings. Once the private sector has established a footing, the government nurseries could concentrate on providing farmers the necessary planting material and extension services at cost. Such a move will draw in additional resources to this critical area and make the government nurseries self-financing.

Other forestry sector activities are under the various projects assisted by outside agencies. These are:

1. Dhamar Agricultural and Forestry Research and Development. This British project has a small forestry component under an expatriate forester. He is conducting trials on shelter belt and terrace woodlot plantations, and runs a nursery producing 150,000 seedlings annually.

2. Tihama Development Authority. The TDA has a forestry component for shelter belts plantation and dune stabilization. Over four years, YR 7.3 million will be spent for technical assistance, training, equipment, civil works and 800 ha. of plantations.

3. Haraz Erosion Control and Afforestation Project. The German government is now implementing a YR 13 million pilot project to revive abandoned terraces, develop farm woodlots, introduce new species and set up an extension service for afforestation, wood utilization and erosion control.

4. Livestock Credit and Processing Project. This project, as part of its range improvement activities, has set up a 150,000 seedling-per-year nursery in Dhamar.

There are five new projects for the ᶜFYP. A YR 33.5 million program, awaiting World Bank appraisal, covers training, nurseries, research, and afforestation of 2000 ha. The Phase III National Agricultural Research Program, just funded by the World Bank, contains a comprehensive forest research component. Besides the normal research activities, the project includes three species-screening sites, establishment of arboreta at the various research centers, and a herbarium. Finally WFP may finance a scheme for planting green belts around major urban areas and UNEP is studying financing of the forestry component of the Al Jawf Rural Development Project worth $5.45 million.

D.   Strategic Considerations

Given the embryonic stage of the Directorate of Forestry and the extreme shortage of trained Yemeni manpower, current and planned activities will exhaust available resources and capabilities. There is also a danger that new projects will divert critical funds from on-going activities. In particular, the existing four nurseries deserve more attention, especially with regard to efficient distribution of seedlings,[3] and careful supervision of plantings by government agencies and farmers to reduce the high rate of die-back. Commercializing these nurseries and bringing in the nations's farmers to the tree nursery business, as recommended, will greatly enhance this essential activity.

Traditional forestry development concepts, although important at this stage, have ultimately a limited scope in Yemen. In an arid region such as Yemen, forest is not a natural climax vegetation, except in a diminutive area where rainfall is adequate. The problems of disappearing natural vegetation, soil erosion, spreading sand dunes, siltation and dropping water tables require an integrated systems approach, combining afforestation, range and watershed management concepts. This is a complicated task, and the necessary techniques are not fully established as far as the YAR'S ecology is concerned. In any case, under the present socio-political arrangement and with a paucity of trained manpower, such a strategy is not yet applicable, although it needs further examining.

The present policy can also be characterized as "top-down" approach, where there is no focus on mobilizing farmers' resources or self-interest. Thus, the richest and most effective sector of Yemeni society seems to be left out. Farmers' self-interest should be co-opted, only because they, and not the government, have the land plus the incentive to do something, at least on abandoned terraces. Also by themselves, government afforestation programs the world over have been totally inadequate to fully satisfy the needs. An approach that fits forestry into the present farming system's croppping and livestock linkages is required, i.e., agro-forestry.

Although some wealthier families in the wettest parts of the highlands do have private woodlots for both conservation and timber, tree planting for other than homestead amelioration is a new concept. After centuries of being used to bountiful nature providing lumber freely, the idea of growing trees as a separate farm enterprise takes time.

Agro-forestry concepts may be the answer whereby plants are introduced that provide fuel, poles, fodder and food as an integral part of the ongoing cropping pattern. Research at ICRISAT in Hyderabad, India, with an ecology similar to the highlands in Yemen, has generated several options. The most promising option is intercropping certain varieties of pigeon-pea with sorghum, Yemen's staple crop. The pigeon-pea, also known as red gram, provides a high quality pulse seed, leaves for fodder, and up to four tons per year per ha. of tall, thin branches suitable for poles and fuelwood. Being a legume, it also fixes nitrogen in the soil, boosting yields of intercropped sorghum by 25-60%. Unlike Acacia cynophylla (Sant, in Arabic), a nitrogen-fixing fodder and timber plant that is the main output of government nurseries, pigeon-pea can be sown directly in the field and does not require one or two special waterings. The plant coppices well, so its branches can be cut twice a year for several years. Thus, it is also ideal for protecting and nourishing terraces too marginal for annual cultivation under sorghum alone.

The Directorate of Forestry is promoting acacia, Eucalyptus camaludensis and E. globulus. The latter are traditional forestry favorites, as they can be grown on very marginal land; however, they do not suit farmers' needs, since seedlings need extra watering and leaves are not edible by livestock. Furthermore, the alkaloids in the leaves of the Eucalyptus do not enrich the soil, but inhibit growth of other plants on the same land.

The pigeon-pea is grown widely in India and Egypt. Globally, twice as much farm land is under this pulse as

under the two eucalyptus species mentioned. CARS has noted
its importance, as food not fuel, and has a few trial plots.
A visit to ICRISAT would be highly profitable for CARS
management and researchers, not only for data on the
pigeon-pea, but also for the work that the institute has
done to improve all aspects of small-scale farmer
productivity in an ecological and social environment similar
to Yemen's.

NOTES

1. Nasser A. Aulaqui, *Household Energy and Tree Seedling Demand Survey in the Southern Uplands of the Yemen Arab Republic.* Sanaa: Sanaa University, June, 1982.

2. Women do not collect firewood and dung everyday.

3. Despite the high demand for seedlings, one-third of all seedlings produced are still in the nurseries awaiting distribution.

XII. FARM SYSTEMS

A. Background

Yemen's farming sector exhibits a number of characteristics that differentiate it from other developing countries. With no currency restrictions, free movement of labor and goods across almost open borders, no subsidies save for some tariff protection, and no government price controls or economic regulations, in eight years rural Yemen has advanced from an under a $1 a day wage economy to a $2 per hour economy, without any serious, wrenching social dislocations that afflict so many other developing countries, whether growing or stagnating. Far from being laid waste by a sudden intrusion of foreign economic forces, rural Yemen is thriving, without having achieved any perceptible technical breakthrough in agricultural productivity.

1. Change Since 1973

The dramatic rise in the oil-based incomes of neighboring countries underpins Yemen's dynamic export-oriented economic growth. The export sector consists almost entirely of just under a million farm households directly exporting the one domestic resource in abundance--unskilled manpower. Over the decade, hundreds of thousands of Yemeni men, unencumbered by migration controls, moved from subsistence labor, worth about YR 3-4 per day for part of the year, to jobs in Saudi Arabia paying YR 100-150 per day. Living frugally, these men could save and remit much of their income in cash and goods directly to their villages. Disposable income of rural families boomed, freeing villagers from sole dependence on subsistence farming and giving them access to a range of goods and services unthinkable a decade before.

2. The Impact of Remittance Income

This inflow of money and goods, averaging $1-2 billion a year, naturally generated dynamic multiplier effects within the rural economy. Since 90% of the total population and the migrant labor force is rural, farmfamilies were the first to benefit from this income flow, and they seem to have benefited fully. This is a rare phenomenon in developing countries where external income benefits, even if based on exports of domestic agriculture, generally trickle down to rural families only after filtering first through the government, urban and foreign service sectors.

The first multiplier impact was rapid inflation. A subsistence economy, after centuries of stagnation, is incapable of responding to a sudden upsurge in demand for its goods and services. Consequently, prices shot up, seemingly to approach levels prevailing in Saudi Arabia. From 1973 to 1978, daily minimum rural wages rose from YR 3-4 to YR

70-80; land values rose a hundred-fold; prices for local legumes, meat and vegetables rose 389%, 495% and 454% respectively; local cereal prices, despite availability of cheap imports rose 160%; and the general price index rose 367% (Table XII-1). The high wages and large cash holdings of the returning migrants were thus rapidly passed on to the rest of the rural society--to whomever had goods, service or assets to exchange. In due course, the multiplier effect passed on to the towns and out of the economy via imports. This in turn benefited government revenue, over 50% of which still comes from import duties and levies, and the urban classes. Their expenditures in turn completed the circular flow of funds back to the agricultural sector, net of leakages, through higher demand for local foods and gat, and development investment in infrasturcture, especially roads. The latter further facilitated farmers' responses to changing market prices and encouraged development of marketing centers for the goods farmers bought and sold.

B.   The Changing System

1.   Developing Trends

As the inflow of remittances began to level off, the inflationary impetus started to decelerate. It is thus possible to discern certain major trends evolving in the rural economy. First, rural incomes have not deteriorated in relation to urban incomes. Unskilled wage rates in the

TABLE XII-1

YEMEN ARAB REPUBLIC

AGRICULTURAL SECTOR MEMORANDUM*

Agricultural Wages and Consumer Price Index

Year	Average Daily Wage (YRls)	Consumer Price Index (Sanaa) 1972 = 100	% Change
1972	2	100	43
1973	3-4	143	27
1974	5-6	181	24
1975	10	224	17
1976	20	261	25
1977	37	326	13
1978	45	367	13
1979	50	477	33

---

* FAO Agricultural Assessment of Yemen
Appendix III - El-Omeri (Draft Report, 1979);
Yemen Arab Republic - Development of a Traditional
Economy, Basic Data, Vol. 1, December, 1978;
International Financial Statistics, Vol. XXXII,
January 1979, pp. 402-403.

highlands are YR 50 per day plus food and _gat_, equivalent
to the urban wage of YR 70 per day. In the Tihama, wages
are sometimes less, usually YR 40 per day plus food and
gat for men. As urban growth has boomed, rural development has more than kept apace, with investments in housing,
water supply, roads, rural trade and transport. Consumer
goods are as abundant in rural households as in the towns,
as almost every village boasts television, electricity,
vehicles and other accoutrements of modern consumer living.

The second major trend is that, although consumer goods
and domestic asset acquisition account for the bulk of the
remittance income, rural household investment has claimed a
healthy portion of expenditure, probably more so than in
urban areas. Villagers have devoted enormous resources on
buildings, orchards, wells, pickups, tractors, commerce and
rural roads or tracks, and this investment is highly
visible.

All these activities, except main roads, have been
financed out of individual or family savings. For
electricity, entrepreneurs have set up village supplies
based on small generators. Village road building is usually
a joint community effort, paid for by direct household
contributions and complementing the efforts of the LDAs.

The third major trend is the persistence of high wage
levels. Yemen is now closely linked to the Saudi Arabian

economy, and so to its price structure. Labor mobility between the two countries provides both a stimulus to Yemen's national income and a floor to local wages; as already mentioned, unskilled rural cash wage rates are YR 50 per day, which on an hourly basis works out at YR 8-15 or $2-3 per hour. Skilled wage rates approximate levels of neighboring countries. For example, almost anywhere in the country, masons earn YR 300-350 per day, carpenters and electricians YR 200-250 per day, diesel mechanics and tractor drivers YR 40-70 per hour. Although no national data on household incomes are available yet, a recent study conducted by Sanaa University in Taiz and Ibb areas on behalf of the Forestry Department revealed a median household income of YR 2000-3000 per month[1] (Tables XII-2 and XII-3). High local wages have encouraged the government to issue temporary work permits for skilled migrant workers from outside Yemen, notably in construction, hotels, government service and commerce. Local income prospects have also encouraged many long-term Yemeni emigrants to return, even from Europe and the U.S. Although they generally do not reside in their tribal villages, these returnees maintain strong family ties and ownership of inherited land.

The fourth major trend comprises a remarkable domestic preference and willingness to pay high premiums for products

TABLE XII-2

AVERAGE MONTHLY INCOME PER HOUSEHOLD*

Amount of Income	Percentage of Households in each Group	
	IBB	TAIZ
Under YR 1000	11	43
1000 - 2000	33	16
2000 - 3000	23	19
3000 - 4000	16	9
4000 - 5000	8	5
5000 and over	9	8

TABLE XII-3

OCCUPATION OF HEADS OF HOUSEHOLDS SURVEYED*

	IDB	TAIZ
Fulltime farmer	66%	43%
Laborer	10%	30%
Farmer-laborer	3%	6%
Immigrant	10%	4.8%
Merchants-shopkeepers	5%	4.5%
Clerks (government, etc.)	1%	7.0%
Miscellaneous	5%	4.7%
Total	100%	100%

* Nasser A. Aulaqui. Household Energy and Tree Seedling Demand Survey in the Southern Uplands of the Yemen Arab Republic. Source: Sanaa University, June, 1982.

of local agriculture, despite abundant availability of cheaper imported alternatives. Nowhere is the impact more apparent than for local foods such as cereals and livestock products. Table XII-4 gives the retail prices of domestic and imported foods in local markets in October-November 1982.[2] Far from suffering from the flood of imports, local products are more than holding their own share of the consumers' expenditures. In effect, there are two distinct markets--one for "cheap" imports and another for "quality" local products. The income benefits accruing to rural households from this market stratification are obvious.

2. Status of Farm Incomes

The above description gives one facet of the macro-economic setting for present-day Yemeni farming. Through exporting their labor and almost fully appropriating the consequent flow of remittance or off-farm income, farm families have increased their disposable incomes enormously. This has freed the rural sector from total dependence on low-level subsistence agriculture, and accelerated its shift to commercialization. Rising incomes in towns and villages have further expanded demand and prices for local foods and other crops. Thus farm incomes continue to rise, and poverty among farmers is minimal, relative to the situation ten years ago and to other developing countries. The high incomes of rural households have enabled many farm families

TABLE XII-4

RETAIL PRICES OF MAJOR FOODS

IN OCTOBER - NOVEMBER 1982*

Commodity		YR/kg or unit noted
Wheat Flour - local		3-5
imported		1.5
Sorghum	- local, different varieties	3-5
	- imported	3
Maize	- local	4
Potatoes		4-5
Okra		10
Onions		5-6
Tomatoes		6-8
Papaya		7-8
Grapes	- different varities	10-20
Raisins		35-60
Oranges	- imported	6
Apples	- imported	8
Bananas	- imported	6
Chicken	- country breeds (live)	30-40
	- local, imported chicks (live)	18-20
	- imported poultry (frozen)	10-15
Mutton		70-80
Goat		40-50
Beef	- local (fresh)	60-80
	- imported (frozen)	25
Eggs	- local (each)	0.6
	- imported (each)	0.5
Fish	- (fresh)	30-80

* Observation in Sanaa, Taiz and local markets near Sanaa.

to invest in productive activities, on-farm and off-farm, be it gat, fruit trees, wells, tractors, pickups or trade.

On the farms themselves, the traditional structure still applies, though gradually adapting to change. Other income sources and the shortage of labor have led to a move away from low productive, rainfed, subsistence cereal farming toward producing high value crops for the market. Thus, rainfed sorghum production has declined and marginal terraces have been abandoned, while production of gat, vegetables and fruits has increased. Production of grain sorghum has stagnated, but the use of sorghum for fodder has increased. Lack of rural manpower has led to more women, especially from poorer families, taking up field work, while permitting women in wealthier rural households to withdraw from subsistence activities. Labor shortages and the rising ability to pay have led to an increase in the use of hired labor and greater recourse to mechanization.

3. Production Practices

Of the total of 10 million ha. of land, 85% is low-grade range. Thus, only 1.ᵣ million ha. are on average cultivable, of which only 250,000 ha. are irrigated in some form; 85% of cropping is still under rainfed conditions.

From a six-province survey, conducted in 1981 by the MAF, it is clear that farms are very small, with two-thirds being under 1 ha. The average household had 5-7 people, two-thirds of whom were in the productive age group, between 11 and 64 years of age. Migrants represented 5.4% of the total population surveyed, or one in five of all males between the ages of 15 and 44. Agricultural work was the main occupation of 92.5% of the total labor force over 10 years of age. About 69% of the men worked fulltime and 18% worked occasionally in agriculture, while only 11% did non-agricultural work. Of the women, 44.6% worked full time and 52.0% worked part time in agriculture. Family labor accounted for all labor input on 60% of the farms, while 30% of the farms relied on hired labor either for ploughing or harvesting.

The prevalent crop in highland rainfed and irrigated areas is sorghum, occupying about 90% of the cropped area. In the drier Tihama, the rainfed crop is millet, undersown with pulses. Livestock is closely integrated into the farming system, as cereal production is as much for fodder as for the grain. Eighty percent of the households surveyed had at least one head of cattle, while 25% of the farmers had sheep and goat herds averaging 22 head.

For cereals, land preparation involves ploughing and working the land several times with oxen in the highlands, but only once or twice by camel in the Tihama. According to the survey, nearly 30% of the farmers use tractors, and one in twelve owns his own tractor. Improved seeds are rarely used, though nearly 45% of the farmers use some fertilizer on 16% of their land, mostly on non-cereal crops. Harvesting is done by hand after the grain has ripened and field-dried. Wheat and barley are threshed by having animals walk over it; sorghum is flailed with sticks.

Total labor input for sorghum and millet is about 45 man-days per ha., 10-33% of which may be hired labor. With this low nonlabor input system, grain yields are also low, averaging 1.0 tons per ha., ranging 0.5-1.5 tons per ha. for sorghum, depending on the water availability. In the Tihama, rainfed yields are only about 0.3 tons per ha. for both sorghum and millet, due to lower rainfall and wider spacing. However, fodder yield is equally important, and a ha. of sorghum will yield two to three times the weight of grain in leaves and stalks, which are fed mainly to farm cattle.

4. Farm Yields and Incomes

The process described accounts for 75-80% of farm field activity. Assuming an average yield of 1 ton of grain valued at YR 2 per kg. and 2 tons of fodder worth YR 1 per kg. (current prices), the gross income is around YR 4000 per ha. Net income would be about YR 3900 per ha, if no purchased inputs are used, but the cost of seed is deducted. For a sharecropper, rent would account for an average 33% of the gross income, and he would also have to pay 10%

zakat (tax), leaving him a net of about YR 2220 per ha.

Herein lies the explanation for the prevailing rural wage rate of YR 40-70 per day. For the sharecropper netting YR 2000 per ha. from a labor input of 45 days, the return per day is YR 44. This opportunity cost is also the market rate. Migration having drained previous surplus labor, the only alternative labor he can hire is another similarly-placed sharecropper, whether male for female. Without the migration safety value, the market rate would be much less. Migration and remittance income, inter alia, boost local demand for food, which, combined with consumer preference for local foods, drive up the price of cereal to YR 2 per kg. ($440 per ton, or $1.2 per bushel), as against YR 1.5 for imported wheat flour[3] in local shops.

Detailed information on costs and returns is available at present only from SURDU. This area is not representative of all the highlands, as it enjoys the highest rainfall, 800-1,200 mm. Table XII-5 gives the per-ha. figures for present conditions without project at 1981 prices, and shows how a representative owner-operated farm of 1.0 ha., with 60% of the area under sorghum, had a gross income of YR 6114 and net income of YR 3171, or about YR 40-45 per day for a total labor input of about 70-80 days. Vegetable profits in this instance are low. In 1981 excess production, primarily of tomatoes, depressed prices--a marketing problem that should be overcome shortly with growing farmer experience and opening up of new markets.

From Table XII-6, it can be seen where the farmers' likely emphasis is going to be. Assuming project success in extension and improved input supply, yields are projected to increase across the board, with farm efforts shifting toward vegetables, fruit, coffee and forage (alfalfa), as is already beginning to happen. At full development, in 1986, the representative 1 ha. farm's gross income is forecasted at YR 21,842 and net income at YR 15,527--up 357% and 490% respectively from the before-project situation. Net income should then approximate YR 150 per labor day at 1981 prices. The farm would be fully market-oriented, with the bulk of the grain being sold, as against the present, where most of it is consumed for subsistence. Consumption of grain for an average family is about one ton of sorghum per year, including some as feed for the family's cow.

What is interesting is the very high net return of YR 122,250 per ha. projected for fruit and YR 49,000 per ha. for alfalfa, albeit from only 10% of the farm area. Vegetables, potatoes and coffee give lower but still lucrative net returns, YR 15,000-36,000 per ha., on an additional 15% of the farm area.

Most farms, however, cannot have 25% of their area under high value crops, since water is limited. Groundwater

TABLE XII-5
SURDP YIELDS AND VALUES
At Present, Without Project, 1981 Prices*

Crop	Area % of farm (1 ha)	Yield ton/ha.	Price YR/ton	Gross Value YR/ha.	YR/farm	Costs YR/ha.	Net Value YR/ha	YR/farm
Sorghum—Grain Fodder	60.0	1.17 4.00	1,800 600	2,106 2,400	1,264 1,440	2,100	2,405	1,444
Wheat —Grain Fodder	4.8	1.25 2.00	1,720 1,000	2,150 2,000	103 96	2,065	2,085	100
Barley —Grain Fodder	3.7	1.3 2.00	1,300 1,000	1,690 2,000	63 74	1,850	1,840	68
Maize —Grain Fodder	13.9	1.76 3.80	1,980 600	3,445 2,280	479 317	2,800	2,925	407
Pulses	8.9	1.5	2,400	3,600	320	2,000	1,600	142
Potatoes	2.3	11.88	2,640	31,360	721	17,000	14,360	330
Vegetables	3.5	9.00	1,600	14,400	504	12,000	2,400	84
Fruit Trees	1.8	8.00	4,375	35,000	630	6,000	29,000	522
Coffee	0.5	0.69	30,000	20,700	104	6,000	14,700	74
Others	0.6							
Total	100.0%				6,115			3,171

* SURDU Monitoring and Evaluation Unit, personal communication.

TABLE XII-6
SURDP YIELDS AND PRICES
At Full Development With Project, 1981 Prices*

Crop	Area % of farm (1 ha)	Yield ton/ha.	Price YR/ton	Gross Value YR/ha.	Gross Value YR/farm	Costs YR/ha.	Net Value YR/ha.	Net Value YR/farm
Sorghum–Grain	40	3.0	1,800	5,400	2,160	2,900	5,500	2,200
Fodder		5.0	600	3,000	1,200			
Wheat –Grain	8	1.7	1,720	2,924	234	2,500	2,420	194
Fodder		2.0	1,000	2,000	160			
Barley –Grain	5	1.5	1,300	1,950	98	2,300	1,650	83
Fodder		2.0	1,000	2,000	100			
Maize –Grain	10	3.9	1,980	7,720	772	3,900	7,820	782
Fodder		6.0	1,000	6,000	600			
Pulses	10	2.1	2,400	5,040	504	2,500	2,540	254
Potatoes	6	18.0	2,640	47,520	2,251	22,000	25,520	1,531
Vegetables	8	25.0	1,600	40,000	3,200	25,000	15,000	1,200
Fruit Trees	5	30.0	4,375	131,250	6,563	9,000	122,250	6,113
Coffee	2	1.5	30,000	45,000	900	9,000	36,000	720
Others	1	–	–					
Forage	5	50.0	1,000	50,000	2,500	1,000	49,000	2,450
Total	100.0%				21,842			15,527

* Ibid.

resources may be approaching the limits of exploitation in some areas already, given the dropping of the water tables in the Sanaa, Dhamar and Tihama plains. The only recourse open to farmers is to reduce the present excessive and wasteful use of water by minimizing distribution losses and field usage. Yemeni farmers are not fully attuned to the need to save water, since irrigated farming for them is merely an extension of rainfed practices where yield is a direct function of water. The potential savings are great, as water application can be cut substantially, depending on crop and local conditions, without affecting yield. Irrigation extension is of prime importance in cases where farmers depend on pumps and already are paying heavily for wasting water.

All food crops, other than sorghum, millet, wheat, barley and pulses, depend on supplementary irrigation. Yet, even with pump irrigation, sorghum is the dominant crop for its relatively high grain and fodder value. In the Tihama, for example, the annual yield from one ha. of pump-irrigated sorghum, from two ratoons, can be three tons of grain plus 10 tons of fodder, giving a gross return today of about YR 16,000 ha. Even a sharecropper, using his own labor and animals, but paying the pump owner half and the landlord one-quarter of the gross, nets YR 4,000 per ha. for very little input other than seed, animal power and family labor.

Other irrigated crops currently grown in the Tihama, and their yields, are as follows:

Maize	Grain	1.2	(tons per ha.)
	Fodder	2.5	
Sesame		1.2	
Tobacco (total plant)		2.5	
Tomatoes		5.0-10.0	
Melons		7.0-10.0	
Cotton		1.0	
Papayas		5.0	
Bananas		7.0	

Alfalfa is being introduced, but few farms have yet supplanted sorghum with it. Citrus, mangoes and guavas also show promise. Farm and budget estimates prepared by the CID Horticultural Project team indicate very high returns on investments in properly developed orchards, with internal rates of return 14%-32% under the most pessimistic assumptions.

In the highlands the favored irrigated crops are qat, alfalfa, grapes, and temperate fruits. Qat has the highest pay-off, with net return anywhere from YR 60,000 to YR 300,000 per ha. It is thus the fastest growing enterprise, replacing sorghum and coffee. MAF estimates that 40-45,000 ha. is under qat, and qat profits, not remittance income, finance 90% of all highland tubewell investment. Grapes are next to _qat_ in profitability. Table XII-7 gives an analysis of gross and net returns for a number of crops, excluding _qat_, calculated in 1979 by a World Bank team.

5. Livestock and Farm Power

As already mentioned, livestock is an integral part of the Yemeni farming system. Caring for cattle, above all, is women's work, but they do not approach it from a commercial perspective. Most animal products, even lambs and kids, are consumed at home and never enter the market. In particular, 80-90% of the milk is used at home, consumed fresh or processed into yogurt, ghee and cheese. In addition to providing family sustenance, the large animals are absolutely essential to farming, providing draft power for land preparation, threshing and transportation.

An estimated 85% of farm holdings surveyed use draft animals for land preparation, while 30% use animals and tractors. The effective horsepower of a pair of oxen or a camel is 0.5-1.0, while that of a pair of donkeys is under 0.5 hp. In a six-hour day, a pair of oxen can plough 0.10 to 0.25 ha, depending on topography. The current hire rate is around YR 200 a day, including operator and feed, but this figure is lower in the coastal region. Tractor hire rates are YR 70-120 per hour, and work rates are very slow,

TABLE XII-7

GROSS AND NET RETURNS PER HA. FOR SELECTED CROPS

Yemen Arab Republic*

Crop**	Years to Full Production	Gross Return	Net Return
Oranges	8	109,200	91,580
Mangoes	10	100,000	83,720
Limes	8	98,000	78,220
Peaches	8	88,200	71,320
Guavas	8	89,600	71,780
Papayas	3	60,000	39,720
Grapes	5	48,000	39,596
Bananas	2	18,200	5,990
Alfalfa	1	53,320	43,875
Tomatoes	1	31,875	19,125
Maize	1	5,040	3,240
Coffee	7	14,000	3,120
Wheat	1	3,640	2,420
Sorghum	1	3,480	2,280

*   Calculated from World Bank, 1979, Tables 15, 16, 39;
CPO, 1981.

**   Crops for which estimates can be found. The conven-
tional wisdom is that returns on qat are significantly higher than for any other crop grown in the YAR.
Chaudry reports a gross return to qat of YR
1,494,000 per ha. based on retail prices. (See
Chaudry, M.A., _Economic Potentials and Import of
Cereals, Fruits and Vegetables in YAR_, MAF, February,
1981). The same report shows gross returns to fruits
several times higher than those reported above. The
World Bank source estimates only a YR 79,500 gross and
a YR 52,150 net for qat. Judgment would suggest the
World Bank figures are too low, while Chaudry's are
perhaps too high.

about 0.2 ha. per hour. The cost, however, of land preparation and planting per ha. with either method is YR 700-
1,300, which is high by international standards. Tractors
cannot be used on steep slopes or terraces, where draft
animals remain supreme.

6. Energy

A household energy survey conducted by Sanaa University
in 1982 estimated average fuelwood consumption at 762 kgs.
per capita. Moreover, fuelwood prices, at an average YR 1
per kg.[4] are among the highest in the world, so that per
capita fuel expenditure is over YR 2 per day. Firewood
accounted for 68% of the family's fuel requirements,
followed by crop residues and dung at 16%, kerosene at 10%
and butane at 6%. Over 80% of the households surveyed had
kerosene or butane stoves in addition to the traditional
tannur oven. Given the high price and shortage of firewood, there presumably is a rapid increase in home use of
petroleum fuels. Continued reliance on traditional cooking
is very expensive; an average family of seven is estimated
to consume daily 14 kgs. of fuelwood, 1-2 kg. charcoal, and
12-15 kgs. dung and crop residues. It is estimated that
20-25% of the average annual family income is spent on purchasing these fuels. Many rural families collect rather
than buy some of their fuelwood. Environmental damage
aside, this requires that women spend four to eight hours on

periodic wood-gathering expeditions, at an approximate opportunity cost of YR 40 per day.

Fuelwood costs come second only to food in total family expenditure of many households.[5] It can only be hoped that market forces will accelerate the move to cheaper kerosene and butane, now becoming available in rural areas. It is hoped, too, that the electricity corporation will advance its investment in rural distribution systems in the near future. With the national electricity grid supplying only 10% of the rural households, most rural electricity depends on small diesel generators with high unit costs. Rural rates average around YR 3 (US$0.66) per kwh, while electricity from the grid currently sells for YR 1.5 per kwh in rural areas, although its long-term costs are YR 1.2 per kwh. The extension of the grid will help bring down other energy costs borne by farmers particularly where they can electrify their diesel powered wells. Electrification, costing YR 4,000 per connection and YR 1.5 per kwh, could reduce recurrent costs of pumping by 50-75% and lead to much lower down-time and repair costs than experienced with diesel prime movers.

7.   Storage and Processing

On-farm storage problems have been examined by FAO, whose field surveys in 1981 indicated that farmers store grain for a very long time--up to eight years. Given the pre-1973 environment of isolated subsistence societies needing to be totally self-reliant, these hoarding instincts are understandable. However, under present conditions of high incomes and abundant grain supply, these attitudes and practices are changing.

Farmers mainly store their grain these days in oil drums and gunny sacks; traditional methods using underground stores, earthenware pots and cane baskets are now a rarity. Sorghum and maize account for 90% of the stored grains and overall, the annual percentage of damage in stored grain varies from 18% to 25%. Insects are the main cause of damage; fortunately, the dry climate minimizes the danger from fungus infestation. The survey does not mention any rodent damage. No pesticides were used, and only 1% of the farmers surveyed mixed wood ash with their grain. Shortening the storage period will reduce storage losses, as will improved storage structures and practices, which are a function of extension a . time. Nevertheless, on-farm losses in storage will decrease, as farmers realize that grain need not be held for more that a few months. Demand exceeds domestic supply, and, providing the government staggers wheat imports to accomodate domestic sorghum entering the market, farmers can readily sell most of their harvest without depressing post harvest prices.

Farmers also suffer heavily from other forms of post-harvest losses. Substantial loss and spoilage occur on the threshing ground, due to birds, trampling, manure, dirt and rodents. Appropriately designed sorghum threshing machines would be the single most important aid in this respect, one that will also reduce the high labor and animal power requirements demanded by traditional methods.

The only important on-farm processing in Yemen is flour milling and drying of fruits. The former is widely dispersed and is now almost totally done by diesel-powered grain mills. These are found in almost every village, run by entrepreneurs charging around YR 3 per 100 kg. Raisins are the predominant dried fruits, produced in a simple process of sun-drying grapes over 40-70 days.

8. Input Supply

The increase in disposable incomes, the spread of the road network and investment in pickups and trucks by rural businessmen have greatly speeded the flow of goods and services to and from the villages. Consumer goods, including imported grain and frozen chicken, are readily available to most villagers in Yemen. The same is the case for farm inputs such as tractors, fertilizer, fuel and implements. The most expensive modern input is tractor power, with an estimated 26% of the farmers already depending on hired tractors for land preparation. Fertilizers, used by 45% of the farmers in the MAF survey, are available for YR 68-72 per 50 kg. bag either by credit through the ACB, or from private traders for cash. Private traders obtain their fertilizers cheaply from Saudi Arabia, where unlike in Yemen, it is sold with heavy subsidies. Diesel pumps have been the most important factor for increased farm production over the past ten years, being the basis of 72,000 ha. now irrigated by wells. Two-thirds of this area may be under qat production.

With the spread of tractors, pickups and pumps, maintaining this mechanical equipment now rates as the most important production problem for farmers. Users are not fully aware of the right way to handle their equipment, especially tractors, so breakdowns are frequent, tying up valuable capital and thus raising costs of farm production. Mechanics are available in most villages, but there is an urgent need for proper training. Still, their costs are high, YR 40-80 per hour. Spares are also very expensive, since dealers do not maintain adequate inventory. Waiting for spares, especially slow-moving ones, ties up mechanics' shop space and repair time, as stripped-down tractors await attention. These problems also apply to pumps and other diesel prime movers.

As farmers invest more and more in mechanical equipment, their maintenance and spare parts problems will get worse. From the farmers' point of view, assistance in mechanical engineering is the most pressing demand, exceeding that for crop advice. Increased supply and reduced cost of maintenance and repair skills would have an immediate and permanent impact on farm incomes by increasing productivity of existing farm capital.

9. Agricultural Credit

Formal credit is limited to areas where development projects are currently implemented. These started in 1974 with the TDA, followed by SURDU in 1976. Credit is supplied as part of the overall extension effort. It is available only for in-kind purchase of fertilizer at an interest rate of 9%.

Interviews with farmers indicate that the availbility of credit is not a problem, and this is confirmed by credit specialists in Sanaa. Migrants' remittances have swelled the incomes of many rural families. If a farmer needs funds to purchase agricultural supplies, rare is he who cannot obtain needed cash from the extended family. Of course, many villagers with small resources would like to buy items such as tractors, pickups or pumps that cost YR 70,000-YR 250,000 and complain of the lack of credit, as does any farmer the world over when faced with such large cash outlays.

Nevertheless, the bottom third or so of the rural
income strata probably do lack the income necessary to buy
essential capital items such as cattle. However, since they
mostly practice traditional agriculture, with its very low
requirement for purchased inputs, there is no shortgage of
draft animals or tractors for rent and financing operacing
costs are not a major problem.

10. Food Consumption and Nutrition

Table XII-8 gives the estimates of per capita consumption of major food items in 1974/76 and 1979/81. The
figures apply to villages as well as towns, since 90% of the
population is rural. The change in consumption habits is
quite dramatic. Consumption of the old staple, sorghum, has
dropped, while that of all other commodites--particularly
quality foods such as vegetables, fruits, meat and eggs--has
risen significantly. Overall, nutrition has definitely
improved; and under-nutrition, reported to affect 9% of the
population in 1974-76, is probably at lower levels today.

The large increase in consumption was possible because
of ability to import. Yemen is self-sufficient in sorghum,
vegetables and fish; imports account for the bulk of the
increased consumption of other foods. The growth of imports
has been most noticeable in poultry and egg consumption, yet
the inflow has not impacted negatively on domestic prices of
meat or eggs, which suffer from an inelastic supply but

enjoy a marked local preference in the short term. Domestic vegetable production has kept pace with the booming demand farmers have been able to increase both quantity and range of vegetables to meet demand. Tables XII-9 and XII-10 give the areas and production of domestic agriculture at the beginning and end of the last plan period, and Table XII-11 gives estimates of labor requirements in agriculture.

11. Health

Next to adequate food, health is the most important pre-occupation of rural families. In the past ten years, it has definitely improved, with a better food supply and higher off-farm incomes to purchase drugs that are now widely available. In addition, expenditures by villagers and the government on improved water supplies and health facilities, plus investment in the roads and vehicles, have improved villagers' access to clean water and medical care.

Ignorance of basic hygiene, sanitation, proper nursing and feeding habits, continues to take a heavy toll on human life, especially on infants and mothers. The health statistics are still bad; infant mortality is still around the highest in the world, between 15.5% and 21.0%, while intestinal parasites and dysenteries affect 85% of the population. The average incidence of bilharzia (schistosomiasis) is 97 per 1,000, going up to 200 per 1,000 in some provinces; while that of tuberculosis and malaria is about

TABLE XII-8

PER CAPITA FOOD CONSUMPTION
Kgs/Year*

	1974-76	1979-81	% Change
Flour-wheat	31.0	43.5	40.3
sorghum/millet	112.6	55.0	-51.2
barley	4.0	3.1	-22.5
Rice	.8	3.2	400.0
Potatoes	9.8	14.5	48.0
Sugar	11.2	16.2	44.6
Pulses	11.5	11.7	1.7
Vegetables (fresh)	27.5	42.4	54.2
Fruits (fresh)	33.9	43.4	28.0
Beef	1.8	2.9	61.1
Mutton	5.3	5.9	1.9
Poultry	0.3	10.0	3,333.3
Eggs	.5	2.2	440.0
Fish	2.0	3.2	160.0

* MAF, working papers.

TABLE XII-9

YAR - CHANGES IN CROPPED AREA DURING FFYP*

Crop	Base Year 1975/76	Fifth Year 1980/81	Change
	-------1,000 ha.------		Percent
Sorghum and millet	1,060	681	-35.8
Maize	24	31	+29.2
Wheat	60	63	+5.0
Barley	53	47	-11.3
All cereals	1,197	822	-31.3
Pulses	76	75	-1.4
Vegetables	20	28.2	+41.0
Potatoes	6.8	10.9	+60.3
Fruits	12.3	14.5	+17.9
Grapes	7.7	11.2	+45.5
Coffee	8.0	7.7	-3.8
Cotton	15.0	5.3	-64.7
Tobacco	4.6	6.1	+32.6
Sesame	9.7	10.2	+5.2
All major crops	1,357.1	991.1	-27.0

* MAF 1981.

TABLE XII-10

YAR - PLANNED CROP PRODUCTION INCREASES FOR FFYP*

Crop	Base Year (1975/76)	Fifth Year 1980/81 Planned	Achieved	Percentage Increase Planned	Achieved
	---------1,000 tons----------			------Percent------	
Sorghum and millet	785	1,042	646	+32.7	-17.7
Maize	35	110	49	+214.3	+40.0
Wheat	62	128	65	+106.5	+4.8
Barley	58	83	48	+43.1	-17.2
All cereals	940	1,363	808	+45.0	-14.0
Pulses	76	105	84	+38.2	+10.5
Vegetables	183	705	261	+285.2	+42.6
Potatoes	76	360	131	+373.7	+72.4
Fruits, including grapes	107	142	144	+32.7	+34.6
Coffee	3.4	4	3.6	+17.6	+5.9
Cotton	13.5	32	5.0	+137.0	-63.0
Tobacco	5.6	8	7.0	+42.9	+25.0
Sesame	5.5	11	6.0	+100.0	+9.1
All crop production YRs**	1,662	N.A.	1,813	N.A.	+9.1

* MAF and FFYP.

** In YR million at constant 1975/76 producer prices from CPO National Accounts Data.

TABLE XII-11

YEMEN ARAB REPUBLIC
AGRICULTURAL SECTOR MEMORANDUM

Estimated Agricultural Sector Labor Utilization
in 1977/78 and Projected Requirements in 1989/90*

	1977/78				Projected 1989/90			
	Area (ha) ('000)	Man-Days (per ha)	Total Man-Days ('000)	Man Years	Area (ha) ('000)	Man-Days (per ha)	Total Man-Days ('000)	Man Years
Cereals								
Sorghum & Millet	922	45	41,490	276,600	1,000	30	30,000	176,470
Maize	64	35	2,240	14,940	100	25	2,500	14,700
Wheat	56	41	2,300	15,330	100	35	3,500	20,590
Barley	60	41	2,460	16,400	40	30	1,200	7,060
Legumes, Vegetables								
Legumes	83	35	2,900	19,330	45	40	1,800	10,590
Green Vegetables	23	150	3,450	23,000	40	130	5,200	30,590
Potatoes	9	101	910	6,070	25	75	1,875	11,030
Fruits, Tree Crops								
Fruits	14	100	1,400	9,330	20	80	1,600	9,410
Grapes	10	150	1,500	10,000	15	140	2,100	12,350
Dates	8	50	400	2,670	5	50	250	1,470
Coffee	8	75	600	4,000	10	75	750	4,410
Industrial Crops								
Cotton	5	75	380	2,530	10	45	450	2,650
Tobacco	6	100	600	4,000	10	70	700	4,120
Sesame	10	35	350	2,330	15	40	600	3,530
Other Crops								
Miscellaneous	52	40	2,080	13,070	65	40	2,600	15,300
Total Crops	1,330	-	63,060	420,400	1,500	-	55,125	324,270

continued /....

Livestock ('000)	No.	Man Yrs/	Man Days	Man Years	No	Man Yrs/	Man Days	Man Years
Chickens	3,170	3	-	9,510	8,000	2	-	16,000
Cattle	1,000	70	-	70,000	800	70	-	56,000
Sheep	3,200	10	-	57,600	4,000	18	-	72,000
Goats	7,400	10	-	133,200	8,000	10	-	144,000
Total Livestock	-	-	-	270,310	-	-	-	288,000
Total Crops and Livestock	-	-	-	690,680	-	-	-	612,270
Unaccounted (rounding)	-	-	-	9,320	-	-	-	12,730
Total Employment in Agricultural Sector				700,000				625,000

* From 1975 Census date, Includes 785,462 distributed by sectors plus a part of the
63,360 of the total labor force reported but not distributed by sectors.
Source: Mission estimates. World Bank. April 1979.

20 to 25 per 1,000. Modernity has its negative impacts, too. There is a shift away from breast-feeding to powdered milk diluted with unhygienic water. Increased consumption of _gat_ by lactating mothers and heavy consumption of sugared drinks and white flour by all social classes are also to be deplored. Nutrition and health education must rate top priority in government plans and should be a permanent feature of all donors and ministries which have responsibility in this area.

C.   Strategic Considerations

The inflow of remittances into Yemen has increased family income levels for virtually all people. A high income elasticity of demand for Yemen's agricultural products caused prices for these products to increase substantially. Farmers responded to these price changes by:

- Changing the composition of production to increase output of higher value crops;

- Investing in infrastructure and farm equipment to increase output and market opportunities;

- Increasing use of farm inputs such as fertilizer, insecticides, seeds and plant material.

However, while there were some increases in yield during the FFYP, particularly for sorghum and millet, yield increases have for the most part been modest or nonexistent. There is   evidence suggesting per-unit costs have increased without increased yields. With stabilization of the inflow of remittances, demand will no longer increase as it has done in the past. Consequently, growth in farm incomes in the future will depend increasingly on raising yields and decreasing per-unit costs of production.

In this context the role of government should be to support activities which will assist farmers to expand output at reduced per-unit costs. This can best be done by providing the following services to farmers:

1. Research

Research and trials to develop new production systems should focus both on improved production patterns integrating crops and livestock, as well as new technological packages. Major emphasis should be directed toward suitability of technological packages, varieties and farming systems developed by national and international research institutions throughout the world.

2. Extension

Current needs of farmers cannot be met through development of a traditional extension service, which would take at least one to two decades to institutionalize throughout Yemen. However, while an extension service is being developed, farmers outside the SURDU and TDA type of projects can still be provided with minimal necessary information by imaginative utilization of modern communications media and by using traditional village leaders as change agents. Besides bringing research to farmers by extension, extension should also bring leading farmers to the research. The CARS at Taiz should consider running a programmed course, including audio-visual aids for large landowners and other members of the rural elite, who can afford to come on their own for 2-3 days at a time.

3. Water Management

Improving on-farm irrigation efficiency appears to be equally urgent and cost effective. Groundwater development is extremely expensive; the average Yemen drilling cost of YR 1,000 ($220) per meter, compares to under $100 elsewhere in the region. Modern distribution techniques are limited. Metal piping is used everywhere, because appropriate PVC is not available. There is little knowledge of furrow or sprinkler irrigation.[6] The government and donors should undertake steps to introduce modern technology and develop adequate marketing channels.

4. Maintenance of Capital Equipment.

Here the critical requirement is for more and better-trained mechanics supported by ample levels of spare parts for pumps, tractors, etc. Training of the necessary skills needs to be expanded in ways which will assure the availability of skilled maintenance and repair personnel at the village level.

5. Infrastructure

Government activities in this area should focus on improving farmer access to markets and increasing human capital at the farm level. Priority should probably go to upgrading farm-to-market roads, which are presently rough jeep tracks in most cases and expanding school and health facilities.

6. Electrification

Rural Yemen has a strong suppressed demand for electricity. This is only partly met by small diesel sets supplying power for lighting at the very high cost of about YR 3 ($0.67) per kwh or YR 15 per light month. Such electricity is too costly to power tubewells; it is also subject to frequent breakdowns. Paradoxically, the public supply has excess generating (150 mw) and primary transmission capacity, but investment in local distribution is deficient. With donor assistance, the government can make a significant contribution to reducing per-unit costs of irrigation from tubewells by accelerating investment in local distribution systems to provide lower cost power (YR 1.5 per kwh) from the grid to farms for pumping systems and other farm equipment.

NOTES

1. $440-$660 per month, or a per capita income of $810 to $1,220 assuming 6.5 persons per family.

2. It should be pointed out that duties on vegetables are 107%, and on imported meat, 17%.

3. Called locally <u>Kanadi</u>, a derivation of Kennedy, from the first flour imports brought into Yemen by USAID in 1963. Almost all the wheat and flour is from Australia and no Canadian flour has been imported.

4. Equivalent to $220 per ton, about the same price as that of fueloil c.i.f. Hodeidah. A fuller discussion on the firewood issue is given in the forestry section.

5. This is probably equal to the amount many male heads of household spend on their own daily <u>qat</u> ration.

6. In the highlands, irrigated farms are small and dependent on relatively small sources of spring or well water. Thus the technology required is not of the type used by TDA, but more of the horticultural garden type, with very short distribution links and intensive application.

XIII. AGRICULTURE MARKETS

A.   Domestic Markets

1.   Background

This section concentrates on marketing aspects of domestic production, and how they are affected by imports. It draws on observations made in October-November 1982, and pertinent reports of the MAF and the World Bank.

There are certain marketing factors currently existing in Yemen that, despite import competition, work in the favor of the farmer. These are:

a. Over 80% of the population still lives in the villages and most of them have their own farms producing staple foods.

b. A great proportion of the nation's cash income is generated by migrants, nearly all of whom come from farm families. This weighs purchasing power for foods in favor of rural areas where the production is.

c. Yemen has emerged from a subsistence economy only in the past 5-8 years. Thus, many families not involved in agriculture still have strong family ties to their villages and direct non-commercial access to farm production. This is even true of the urban middle classes for whom ownership of farm land is economically and socially important.

These factors explain why marketed consumption of grain

is only 15% of total domestic production. In the case of meat, butter and ghee, cheese and yoghurt, non-marketed share of output for consumption accounts for 53%, 82% and 88%, respectively. Only for fruits, vegetables and fish does the market account for the bulk of domestic production (Table XIII-1).

d. Rural cash incomes from remittance earnings have enabled many villagers to purchase pickups. Combined with the network of roads and jeep tracks that now connect nearly all villages, farmers enjoy a degree of mobility and access to market centers unmatched in many other developing countries. Nowhere is this more telling than in the distribution of qat, picked fresh early each morning in the highland fields and immediately marketed all over the country. In fact, the qat distribution system provides a crucial commercial network throughout the land, carrying produce to villages on the back-haul and financing considerable new transport capacity through its profits.

e. The final major factor is the pronounced local preference for domestically produced foods. This presents farmers with an expanding demand and premium prices for their products, despite abundant availability of imported alternatives. Rather than destroying the market for domestic produce, imports create a floor to domestic prices. This, plus qat, pushes up gross rural sector incomes, as

TABLE XIII-1

ESTIMATED PROPORTION OF DOMESTICALLY PRODUCED SELECTED

AGRICULTURAL COMMODITIES TRADED VIA MARKET CHANNELS,

1976/77, 1980/81 and 1986*

Commodity	Percentage of Total Production by Weight		
	1976/77	1980/81	1986
Sorghum	15	10-15	10-15
Millet	5-10	5-10	5-10
Wheat	5-10	5	5
Maize	70	75	80
Pulses	50	60	70
Potatoes	70	85	85
Tomatoes	70	85	90
Vegetables, excluding Potatoes and Tomatoes	65	75	85
Grapes, Fresh	85	90	95
Grapes, as Raisins	80	80	80
Fruits, excluding Grapes and Raisins	50	60	70
Dates	80	80	80
Liveestock, Cattle Sheep	45	50	55
Poultry	50	60	80
Eggs	15	20	40
Milk	7	2	5
Fish	50	70	95
Cotton	75	75	75
Coffee	90	85	75
Tobacco	90	95	95

* J. Allchin, "Marketing and Related Topics", in IBRD. Agricultural Sector Study, November, 1981. Annex I, p. 23.

a proportion of national incomes, to enviable levels by world standards.

An example of how farmers benefit from a combination of imported supplies and local preference is the price relationship between imported wheat and domestic sorghum. The former is priced cif. at about YR 0.90 per kg. (US $200 per ton). Its current, unsubsidized, controlled, retail price throughout the country is YR 1.5 per kg. The consumer prefers the local sorghum and is prepared to pay a premium for it, hence the minimum price goes up to YR 2 per kg. for the cheapest variety of sorghum. Since much of marketed local sorghum is sold directly by farmers to consumers, farmers generally receive this price. Another reason for the high sorghum price at farmgate is that there are no local oligopolistic buyers able to exercise their market power over a mass of financially-weak farmers. Farmers have cash reserves as a cushion while government policy is neutral. Apart from controlling the price of imported grain via regulations setting strict marketing margins on its distribution, the government does not attempt to subsidize local grain, nor does it try to set prices for it.

In effect, there are two distinct food markets, a highly structured one for imported commodities and a free, more informal one for local products. A liberal government policy, far from suppressing producer prices, actually provides a high, almost guaranteed, minimum price for domestic producers, who are the majority of the consumers anyway. In the case of vegetables, government further assists by shutting out imports via a 107% duty. Fresh fruit imports carry a duty of 27%.

2. Produce Marketing

With their large cash holdings from off-farm incomes, Yemeni farmers have substantial marketing power. High demand provides a ready market for their products, while remittances free them from the necessity of having to sell production at harvest time for glut prices to meet living costs and debts. This high cash availability, the ubiquity of pickups in the villages and the ample supply of a vast range of consumer goods in the towns make marketing an attractive activity. Permanent shops have sprouted up rapidly in the countryside, along road junctions, gas stations and in large villages, replacing the weekly itinerant fairs. These enterprises, well financed from remittance savings. further expand the outlets for marketing by the farmer. Table 2 shows how well producers have penetrated the marketing system, proving that many of them have resources to indulge in petty trading.

In terms of volume, sales of fruits and vegetables now outweigh sales of grain, and since produce sold must be fresh, there are now several marketing issues. While only

15% of the grain is traded, fruits and grapes are produced almost entirely for the market, as indicated in Table XIII-2. It can be seen that for tomatoes and grapes, which account for half of total volume fruit and vegetables sales, a substantial part of the produce marketing by farmers is done directly in urban centers. The five top urban centers account for 70% of the national urban market.

Live animals are sold individually or, in the case of sheep and goats, in very small lots. They are traded on-farm or at public markets in the country, with two-thirds of the sales to butchers being made directly by farmers. Prices are privately negotiated between the farmer and butcher, without recourse to weights or grades. Except in four modern abattoirs, butchers slaughter the animals on the

---

TABLE XIII-2

PERCENTAGE (BY WEIGHT) OF MARKETED PRODUCTION
Traded by Producers at Different Locations, 1980/81*

Commodity	On Farms	At Local Centers	At Urban Centers
Tomatoes	5	50	45
Potatoes	25	55	20
Other Vegetables	15	55	30
Grapes, fresh	15	15	70
Grapes, as raisins	0	10	90
Dates	25	55	20
Other fruits	40	50	10

* Ibid., p. 5.

open ground, so hygiene standards are non-existent. Meat is sold warm, and the price is the same for meat, fat, offal and bones. At retail, beef is sold by the kg., while sheep and goats are generally bought live from the butcher, who then slaughters them. Table XIII-3 gives the volumes of selected local and imported livestock products consumed in 1978/79.

Fish is caught in the Red Sea by some 3,000 fisherman who sell at local auctions. Sales are made in bundles of differing sizes, by species, without weighing. Sales records are maintained by species, bundles, price and seller. All transactions are for cash. The auctioneers charge 5-10% commission and may provide credit to fishermen for purchase of gear and supplies, recovering the loans from the auction sales. Table XIII-4 gives the distribution of fish for 1978/79.

Dealers transport fresh fish with ice in large galvanized iron boxes mounted on pickups. At the major towns sales are also made through auctions and by the bundle, although large fish are sold individually. There is no shortage of ice either at the landing sites or in the major towns, but clean facilities at the auctions and retail outlets are lacking; fish are simply traded over a concrete or dirt floor.

TABLE XIII-3

CONSUMPTION OF SELECTED LIVESTOCK PRODUCTS

1978/79*

-----------------------Quantities in MT--------------

Commodity	Domestic Production	Imports	Total Consumption	Home (non marketed) Consumption	Quantit Traded
Red Meat					
(total)	36,950	6,100	43,050	19,950	23,10
Poultry meat	2,600	40,000	42,600	1,200	41,40
Eggs (in					
millions)	201	150	351	170	18
Butter and ghee	3,200	3,400	6,600	2,800	3,80
Cheese and					
Yoghurt	2,000	400	2,400	1,750	65

* Ibid, p. 8.

TABLE XIII-4

DISTRIBUTION OF FISH 1978/79**

Form	Final Consumption	M
Fresh	Coastal	2,50
	Tihama	2,00
	Highlands	2,00
	Saudi Arabia	1,50
Subtotal		8,00
Dried and Salted	All areas	9,50 (fresh equi
Total		17,50

** Ibid., p. 9.

3. Prices and Marketing Margins

Table XIII-5 gives the level of retail prices of selected foods in October-November 1982. The high prices of much of the local produce are evident. Sorghum and wheat sell for YR 3-5 per kg. (US $660-1100 per ton). Nowhere else in the world are free market grain prices so high; Japanese and Saudi Arabian government procurement prices are slightly higher, but only because of massive government subsidies.

The differential in meat prices is even greater. Local free-range chickens sell for YR 30-40 per kg. ($6.60-$8.80), three times more than imported frozen poultry and twice the price of live poultry grown from imported chicks and feed. Fresh beef and mutton sell for YR 60-80 per kg., three times the imported frozen cost. Fish, too, is expensive, selling for YR 30-80 per kg., depending on the species.

It is difficult to generalize on marketing margins, since so many farmers sell directly to retailers. Table XIII-6 gives the shares at three levels of exchange as estimated by CARS. Table XIII-7 gives some prices and margins that prevailed in 1981, analyzed by a marketing expert of the World Bank. A British consultant analyzing the vegetable market structure in the five principal cities estimated that farmers received an average 30-40% of the retail price for tomatoes, potatoes and onions, when they

TABLE XIII-5

RETAIL PRICES OF MAJOR FOODS IN OCTOBER 1982*

Commodity		YR/kg
Wheat Flour	-local	3-5
	-imported	1.5
Sorghum	-local, different varieties	3-5
	-imported	3
Corn	-local	4
Potatoes		4-5
Okra		10
Onions		5-6
Tomatoes		6-8
Papaya		7-8
Grapes	-different varieties	10-20
Raisins		35-60
Oranges	-imported	6
Apples	-imported	8
Bananas	-imported	6
Chicken	-country breeds, live	30-40
	-local, imported chicks, live	18-20
	-imported poultry, frozen	10-15
Mutton		70-80
Goat		40-55
Beef	-local, fresh	60-80
	-imported, frozen	25
Eggs	-local, each	0.6
	-imported, each	0.5
Fish		30-80

---

*   Observations in Sanaa, Taiz and local markets in Sanaa
    area.

TABLE XIII-6

ESTIMATES OF SHARE OF FINAL PRICE OF SELECTED LOCAL ITEMS

ACCRUING TO FARMERS, WHOLESALERS, AND RETAILERS*

Commodity	Share of Final Price %		
	Farmer	Wholesaler	Retailer
Grains	65-75	15-20	10-15
Meat	85-90	-	10-15
Grapes	45-60	10	35-40
Bananas	50-65	-	35-50
Papayas	30-40	10-20	40-60
Vegetables	50-60	10-20	30

* MAF, Agriculture Research Service, various reports.

TABLE XIII-7

AVERAGE PRICES AT THREE MARKET LEVELS FOR DOMESTICALLY

PRODUCED FRUITS AND VEGETABLES

DECEMBER THROUGH APRIL 1980/81**

Commodity	Retail Market Location	Average Prices and Percentages Shares of Consumer Prices					
		Farmers*** To Traders/ Wholesalers		Traders/ Wholesalers To Retailers		Retailer to Consumer	
		YR/kg	%Share	YR/kg	%Share	YR/kg	%Share
Tomatoes	Hodeidah	1.40	23.8	2.24	14.3	5.88	61.9
Tomatoes	Sanaa	3.28	42.1	6.05	35.6	7.79	22.3
Potatoes	Dhamar	2.68	56.4	3.80	23.6	4.75	20.0
Papayas	Taiz	1.95	48.4	-	-	4.03	51.6
Grapes (white)	Sanaa	12.21	64.6	13.75	8.2	18.89	27.2
Grapes (black)	Sanaa	8.12	53.4	9.82	11.5	15.22	35.1
Bananas	Taiz	2.25	39.4	-	-	5.71	60.6

** J. Allchin, op. cit., p. 25.
*** For five of the seven items listed, sales were made between farmer and trader/wholesaler. Papayas and bananas were sold by farmers directly to retailers.

are sold ex-farm. In any case, compared to almost any place else, Yemeni farmers receive a very high percentage of the retail price.

Despite the farmer's marketing strength, prices do vary considerably from place to place during the same time period. Village-to-urban differentials exist, because there is no nationwide system to market intelligence. Also, in the case of tomatoes, there is considerable distortion in the chain from farmers to retailers. At the end of October 1981, for example, retail prices per kg. of tomatoes were YR 6-8 in Sanaa and YR 5 in Taiz, while producer prices were as low as YR 1 for some farmers. Without minimizing the problems farmers face, marketing issues must be seen in the overall context of a predominantly rural economy, with only 15% of the population in the towns. In both the highlands and the Tihama, vegetables are grown and marketed where the population is, although areas with better resources and climate may produce a greater percentage of output for the market.

The establishment of a market information service should be the first priority for the newly created Marketing Department of the MAF. Data collection should be very easy as open air wholesale markets exist in the three major cities, with commission agents who specialize in specific commodities for a 5% fee. The Marketing Department could apply in these markets the same system already in force at the coastal fish markets and broadcast the essential data every morning.

4.   A g r o - I n d u s t r i a l   P r o s p e c t s

Processing of agricultural raw materials is still mostly a village-based activity. Modern agro-industry is at an embryonic stage of development in Yemen, presently consisting or ice cream, flour milling, baking, biscuits, confectionary, vegetable oil, ghee, dairy products, textiles and tobacco. Most of these depend almost on imported raw materials. Domestic resource-based industries are limited to cotton, mineral water and hides and skins.

At present, no vegetable, fruit or fish processing exists on an industrial scale. Yemen's current irrigated area of 250,000 ha is probably too small to generate the required surplus at a low enough price to make industiral processing viable. The potential fresh market is large enough to absorb most if not all the domestically produced fresh vegetable and fruits for at least the next five years. With the recent completion of the coastal road to the Saudi Arabia border, the fresh market will expand even more. These markets should be big enough to underwrite rapid growth in market gardening. As a rule, producing for the fresh market provides the highest returns; processing only becomes viable when production exceeds demand and prices drop.

The Red Sea fisheries are projected by the government to have a sustainable yield of nearly 30,000 tons. FAO experts believe that this figure is too optimistic, since the resource base is poor and no inventory study exists to support the projected tonnage. Furthermore, it is likely that the 1978/79 estimate of 9,500 tons (fresh equivalent) of salted and dried fish is overstated. The public sector plans for export-oriented fish canning and freezing plants, planned for 1984, appear unrealistic. Not only is the availability of fish doubtful, but in an environment where fresh fish prices are among the highest in the world, there is no economic rationale for turning high-value fresh fish into a lower-value processed product competing at international prices. As with vegetables, processing can only be attempted when fresh supply exceeds demand and prices drop to a fraction of their current level.

Increased hide and skin production does not seem promising when the tannery at Taiz is operating at only 25% of capacity. It seems that the livestock numbers are not able to support a higher output, although only an estimated one-third of the available skins are collected each year. Obviously, the hides and skins industry needs close investigation to identify constraints and opportunities.

Agro-industries based on imported raw materials offer much better prospects as already shown by the biscuit factory, for example. One of the most promising would be an oil-crushing and feed-mixing plant, based on imported oil seeds and grain.[1] With imports of poultry, eggs, refined oil and poultry feeds running at over YR 800 million per year, demand growing and the local poultry industry expanding at an annual rate of 60%, Yemen can probably support two or more plants. U.S. industry has the required know-how, and appropriate contacts between American and Yemeni business groups should be encouraged.

Another potential project would be two or three poultry breeding enterprises to supply locally hatched day-old chicks to replace those now flown in from Europe. Since USAID is already supplying assistance to a poultry project, the involvement of U.S. business in at least one hatchery would complement this activity.

A third prospect is for a sawmill totally based on imported logs. Yemen's commercial forestry resources are non-existent, and the few trees it has are rapidly disappearing to meet the insatiable demand for fuel and lumber. Lumber imports presently exceed YR 400 million and per capita consumption, estimated at 2 cubic meters, is still rising. Timber is very expensive and firewood prices are about the highest in the world, YR 800 per cubic meter in the highlands.

A sawmill would meet the growing demand for lumber,

furniture, boxes, poles, etc. Above all, the local firewood
and charcoal market would generate profits from mill wastes.
Generally speaking, mills obtain 60% marketable lumber from
logs. The other 40% is mostly discarded or burnt. With the
high price of fuelwood locally, no part of the log need be
wasted. Although current Yemeni demand is mainly for
tropical hardwoods, softwood consumption is growing and the
U.S. is the world's largest exporter of softwood logs.
Aside from its commercial viability, a local sawmill based
on imported logs would be a most important element in the
preservation of Yemen's trees by increasing the supply of
fuelwood. It would also help reduce household energy costs,
which now claims 20 to 25% of the average family income.

The SFYP lists the following agro-industrial projects
for implementation:

a. Public sector: Tomato paste, fish freezing and
canning, cotton ginning, textiles and pesticides. Except
for pesticides, none of these appear viable. As noted
above, tomato and fish processing are not appropriate, given
current fresh market prices. As noted in Chapter XII,
farmers will probably not grow more cotton since other crops
generate more profits. Yemen cannot compete in textiles
with Asian imports, especially those that come across the
Saudi Arabian border, and consumers have not shown a
preference for locally made industrial textiles.

b. Private sector. Macaroni, vermicelli, grain milling, biscuits, soft drinks, concentrated feeds, starch and glucose from millet, tanneries, shoes and leather. The last three would seem doubtful. Local millet is much too expensive to convert into starch, while imports are so cheap. As noted above, tanneries are not practical. Similarly, shoes cannot be produced at prices competitive with imports.

B. Import and Export Markets

1. The Structure of the International Marketing Sector

YAR importers and exporters ("traders") in any particular commodity line, e.g. agricultural machinery and equipment, are small in number. They are often family-owned, closed corporations. They conduct business operations as one would expect of members in a tight knit oligopoly, realizing that they are highly visible to their competitors and to the total economy.

Retailers of imported consumer goods, on the other hand, are numerous and relatively homogeneous. They are essentially price takers, not price makers. Marketing margins appear to be high and prices standardized. There does not appear to be much incentive to engage in price competition or to take advantage of locational or service factors which might allow differential pricing (i.e., monopolistic competition).

The oligopolistic nature of the import market is

illustrated by the following structural statistics. Five importers dominate the commercial market for imported cereals, the largest with 50% -60% of the market.[2] About 18 machinery manufacturers sell their products in YAR, with five companies accounting for most of the tractor and implement imports.[3] In the frozen poultry market, one firm is responsible for 20% of the imports (1100-1500 MT/month, from France), one-fourth of which is retailed by the importer, the remainder being wholesaled to other Sanaa retailers.[4]

Import licenses are issued by the MST. Committee approval is required for import licenses for wheat, flour, sugar, rice and cement,[5] although one report states that "in practice the commercial import volume of grain is not controlled" because both import licenses and authorization to buy foreign exchange are freely given.[6] Import licenses are issued automatically for other commodities "unless the market is full." After the MST has issued the import license, the Central Bank authorizes the purchase of foreign exchange. Following approval by the Ministry of Industry, a letter of credit is issued by a commercial bank and tenders are offered to bidders.[7]

At least four YARG agencies are involved in the import market. Tenders for wheat and flour go out through a public corporation (GCFT) and private importers. Imports are allocated 60% to private firms and 40% to GCFT.[8] The Government Employee Society and the Military and Police Corporation import foodstuffs, including live animals, for schools, hospitals and the armed forces, but also to sell to the public. The CACB distributes much of the imported agricultural production inputs, discussed in the following section.

Government influences the price of food grains and flour through the activities of its agencies described above. Applying prescribed margins, the MST fixes a maximum price for each imported lot's sale by the importer, wholesaler and retailer. The prices include transport costs and thus vary depending on distance from the port of entry, Hodeidah. Two study teams found that the maximum prices were reasonably effective, strictly at the importer and wholesale levels, partially at the retail level.[9] No official regulation exists in marketing domestic grains.

The Government Employee Society and the Military and Police Corporation, by selling to the public at near cost, often set the market price for the respective imported food commodities and undersell the domestically produced counterparts. The CACB is in a position to monitor and perhaps influence the prices of agricultural production supplies through control of distributi .

-272-

TABLE XIII-8

MAJOR FOOD AND AGRICULTURAL IMPORTS AND EXPORTS

YAR (1980)*

Commodity	Value (1,000 YR)	% of Total Imports
A. Imports		
Live Animals	60,569	0.7
Meat and Meat Products	208,099	2.5
Dairy Products and Eggs	473,971	5.6
Fish and Fish Products	36,352	0.4
Cereals and Products	395,788	4.7
Vegetables and Fruits	538,457	6.4
Sugar and Products and Honey	363,002	4.3
Coffee, Tea, Spices	59,663	0.7
Animal Feedstuffs	36,128	0.4
Miscellaneous Foodstuffs	40,534	0.5
Total: Food and Live Animals	2,212,563	26.2

Commodity	Value (1,000 YR)	% of Total Exports
B. Exports		
Live Animals	656	1.3
Fish	1,704	3.9
Biscuits	18,755	38.3
Potatoes	300	0.6
Fruits	761	1.6
Coffee	879	1.8
Hides and Skins	6,237	12.8
All Other Exports	19,497	39.7
Total: Exports	48,789	100.0

* Central Bank of Yemen, Financial Statistical Bulletin, January-March, 1982, Vol. 10, No. 1.

2. Recent Trends in Import and Export Marketing

Total recorded imports by the YAR were YR 8.454 billion ($1.88 billion) in 1980 and YR 7.868 billion ($1.75 billion) in 1981. For the first three months of 1982 the figure was YR 2.2 billion, but the total for 1982 is expected to be about YR 8 billion.[10] Food product and agricultural imports in 1980 are shown in Table XIII-8. Total exports in 1980, (excluding re-exports), were YR 48.8 million ($10.8 million).[11] Agricultural and food exports constituted 65% of all exports.

For the time period covered by the FFYP (1975/76-1980/81) imports increased at an annual compounded rate of 18.4% in real volume, going from 38% of GDP in 1975/76 to 66.4% in 1980/81. In 1982 the structural composition of imports was:

> 19.8% capital goods
>
> 29.7% intermediate goods
>
> 50.5% consumer goods.[12]

In the judgment of a commercial banker, imports of capital goods, primarily machinery, by the private sector have now stabilized and perhaps declined, while those of the government have increased; thus, the net capital goods imports are at about the same level as in recent years. Capital imports for agriculture should accelerate, if the 30% of total investment scheduled for agriculture in the

TABLE XIII-9

IMPORT DEPENDENCY FOR SELECTED FOODS, 1981*

Food Commodity	Approximate % of Consumption which is Imported
Poultry Meat	90
Wheat	80
Dairy products	50
Sesame	50
Eggs	40
Beef	20

* Mustafa El Mubasher, Study of the Possibilities of Substituting the Imported Agricultural Foodstuff by Domestic Production in the YAR undated ms. in Sanaa.

SFYP is realized.

Exports grew 12.5% annually from 1975/76 to 1980/81, constituting 4.3% of GDP at the beginning of the period and 5.9% at the end.

Estimates of import dependency for basic food commodities in 1981 range from 90% for poultry meat and 80% for wheat to 40% for eggs and 20% for beef (Table XIII-9).

Import duties on the three food products, wheat, flour, and powdered milk are zero and relatively low on most other foods. The notable exception is fresh vegetables, which have a customs duty of 100% plus the combined defense and statistics levy of 7%. However, the YAR is now considered to be fully self-sufficient in fresh vegetable production. Import duties on selected food commodities, as of September 1981, are recorded in Table XIII-10.

Data on imports of agricultural production inputs are sparse and of questionable accuracy. The best available data are given in Table XIII-11.

An important aspect of the agricultural input market is the activity of the CACB, a YARG entity. This is the only institutional source of credit for Yemeni farmers, since commercial banks do not lend to agricultural producers.

CACB is engaged in a major activity of supplying in-kind to farmers, fertilizers, plant protection chemicals, agricultural implements and other crop inputs. CACB entered

TABLE XIII-10

DUTIES LEVIED ON SELECTED IMPORTED AGRICULTURAL

COMMODITIES*

(As of September 10, 1981)

Commodity	Customs	Defense	Type of Duty Statistics	Total
	-Percentage ad-valorem c.i.f.**----			
Meat, Red-frozen	10	5	2	17
Meat, Poultry-frozen	15	5	2	22
Eggs	1	5	2	8
Milk, Powder	NIL	NIL	NIL	NIL
Milk, Fresh, Evaporated, etc.	10	5	2	17
Butter	5	5	2	12
Margarine/Edible Oils and Fats	25	5	2	32
Cheese, White	5	5	2	12
Cheese, Other	25	5	2	32
Wheat, Grain	NIL	NIL	NIL	NIL
Wheat, Flour and Meal	NIL	NIL	NIL	NIL
Sugar	13	5	2	20
Rice	8	5	2	15
Vegetables, Fresh	100	5	2	107
Vegetables, Canned	25	5	2	32
Apples, Fresh	20	5	2	27
Bananas, Fresh	20	5	2	27
Grapes, Fresh	20	5	2	27

Reproduced from IBRD Agricultural Sector Study, November 17, 1981

To express the c.i.f. value in YRs, a conversion rate of $1 = YR 5.00 is used; consequently, the rates of duty tabulated above are increased by the factor $\frac{5.00}{4.50}$

TABLE XIII-11

IMPORTS OF AGRICULTURAL INPUTS, 1976-1980*

Commodity			1976	1977	1978	1979	1980
A. Chemical Fertilizers							
Nitrogen	YR	1,000	-	-	3,917	-	7,361
Phosphate	YR	1,000			32	2,497	140
	MT					15	91
Potash	YR	1,000				18	39
	MT					9	22
Other	YR		2,968	5,069	5,219	28,964	3,311
	MT		4,326				
B. Agricultural Machinery							
Tractors	YR	1,000	699	58,483	71,509	12,745	60,552
	No.					4,284	
Tractor Parts	YR	1,000	2,736	4,378	21,992	36,901	
Carts	YR	1,000	32,670	11,393	928	37,943	16,834
	No.			8,089	23,553	7,912	13,440
Ag. Machinery	YR	1,000	1,975	808	25,550	29,925	13,440
Irrigation							
Pumps	YR	1,000	17,750	48,826	-	43,330	96,836
	No.					55,491	44,932
C. Insecticides, Animal Feeds, Planting Material							
Insecticides	YR	1,000	6,526	3,761	20,862	31,533	23,721
Animal Feeds	YR	1,000	57	1,192	1,355	6,251	34,181
Seeds	YR	1,000	1,737	299	2,187	1,702	1,546
Seedlings	YR	1,000	314			104	450

* All 1977 data are for the last six months only.

Source: A foreign trade publication on Agricultural Materials and Supplies, 1971-1980, Ministry of Agriculture and Fisheries 1982 (Arabic).

into the supply of inputs in-kind in order to ensure that the inputs would be available and that the prices to the farmers would be reasonable. Many traders in the private sector, who originally marketed fertilizers, discontinued as the volume left after CACB operations was too small and the profit margin nonexistent. As a result, only CACB supplies were available in many areas and farmers who were not borrowers from CACB are unable to get supplies, or only a limited amount from bank stocks.[12]

According to personnel at the bank, they offer no advice or guidance to borrowers on the most suitable size or type of the some 50 makes and models of tractors which are imported.[13] As of January 1, 1983, the CACB will discontinue its trading activities, except for fertilizer distribution in remote areas. Private dealers bringing in fertilizer from Saudi Arabia, where its retail price is heavily subsidized, have already started to sell to farmers at prices slightly below those charged by the CACB.

3. Future Indications for Imports and Exports.

a. Pressures on consumer demand for food. The annual rate of growth in food demand was from 3.9% to 6.7% between 1975/6 and 1980/81, taking into account the 1975/81 population increase, domestic food production increase and income growth.

The marginal rate of food self-sufficiency, i.e., the

rate of growth in domestic food production in relation to the rate of growth in demand, for the 1975-81 period was between 18% and 29%. Population and income growth were exerting pressure on food demand from three and one-half to five and one-half times the rate that domestic agricultural production was responding. The impact on food prices and import demand for food is obvious.

The MAF has made preliminary estimates by commodity for food production, imports and consumption at time intervals to the year 2000, along with self sufficiency ratios. In addition to imprecise population and per capita consumption data, food import statistics are uncertain because: (1) CPO figures are derived from import duty collections and are recorded in YR, not physical volume, (2) MST records are higher than CPO's for import licenses issued, which may be executed in a later accounting period, or not at all.

4.   Exports

Exports traditionally have been hides and skins, coffee and cotton. They have declined, and efforts by the government to revive them are unlikely to succeed. Hides and skins exports, generally of poor quality because of low animal nutrition and health, have fallen because livestock numbers have been diminished by drought and disease. They will pick up only as the herds build up, and quality can only improve with increased attention to health and nutrition by farmers. This is a long-term development; in the short term, modern abattoirs, with their more efficient methods, should be able to provide the Taiz tannery with cleaner skins free of flaying damage.

Coffee is now grown almost entirely for domestic consumption. Production is stagnating, mainly because the farm-level technology has not improved at all, and because the same land under _qat_ will give returns many times that of coffee. International coffee price projections are not good, but within Yemen, local coffee has an assured market, selling for about YR 30 per kg. unhusked. This is far above world prices, currently averaging YR 15 per kg. of husked _Arabica_ berries. The Yemeni farmer, however, has an additional incentive in the domestic market in that the husk sells for the same price as the bean. Elsewhere the husk is of no value at all. YAR actually imports coffee husk from East Africa.

Cotton probably has the least prospects. Short-stapled and grown in the Tihama, it must have irrigation; currently yields of seed cotton are 1 to 1.5 tons/ha. This is sold to the state-owned mill, and farmers received about YR 2 per kg. net. Domestic mill demand exceeds production, so additional cotton is imported. Past problems with termites and excessively low prices offered by the mill are now over, but even with more water and extension, production prospects must be deemed dull. With high domestic demand for fodder, fruits and vegetables, farmers obtain much higher returns per ha. and per labor unit growing these other crops instead of cotton.

The most important development affecting Yemen's merchandise exports is the building of the coastal road to join the Saudi Arabian market network. This link was opened in late October 1982. Trucks can now drive all the way from Sanaa or Taiz to Jeddah within three days, opening up a very large and favored market to Yemen's horticulturalists. Exports of melons, okra, tomatoes and other produce should pick up smartly. Transport is available as trucks bringing cargo to Yemen currently return empty. Given this development, it is likely that the proposed tomato plant will not be able to operate profitably because of a lack of raw materials at reasonable prices. It is doubtful that the plant could compete against the fresh market even during the winter glut season.[13] Rather than trying to salvage this doubtful investment, it is probably more remunerative for government to assist in developing the fresh vegetable and fruit market in Saudi Arabia. The immediate and most urgent need is to introduce proper grading and packaging standards and practices. Failure to do so will ensure that Yemeni producers will rapidly be shut out of the sophisticated Saudi Arabian market, a fate already threatening current exports of okra which are shipped ungraded and in sacks.

-282-

5.   The Role of the YARG in Food and Agricultural Imports and Exports.

Government planning in a market oriented economy, where most investments and expenditures are made by private decision makers, can only be indicative of the future direction of the economy. The 1% annual growth rate for imports for the SFYP (1982-86) appears wholly unrealistic, since imports increased more than 18% annually in real volume from 1975/6 to 1980/81.

The SFYP calls for the structure of imports in 1986 to be capital goods, 21%; intermediate goods, 39%; consumer goods, 40%. This is basically a shift of 10% of total imports from consumer goods to intermediate goods, compared to the 1982 import composition cited earlier. In the agricultural sector, this would entail the importation of increased amounts of fertilizers, chemicals, foodstuffs, seeds, plant materials and other expendible inputs to boost domestic production of food and fodder. The present economic and political environment is conducive to intensified productivity in the private sector and will bring this about.

6.   Import-Export Policy Alternatives

The options available to the YARG in manipulating import-export policy are limited for at least two reasons. First, it is contrary to YARG philosophy to intervene in the economic activities of the private sector.[14] Second, in most cases the YARG does not have the means of carrying out interventionist policies. It has neither the manpower, financing nor experience to enforce additional regulations or even stricter adherence to existing ones. An example is import duties, for which no means of collection exists for imports from the YAR's two neighbors, Saudi Arabia and the PDRY.

The following section enumerates and evaluates several policies involving import-export activities which the YARG might consider undertaking. The overall goal is to assist in the development of human capital and social institutions to harmonize the Yemeni economy with that of the outside world.

a. Encourage the importation and local production of appropriate agricultural technology. This includes developing ways for stimulating private sector demand for adaptable crop varieties, tractors and implements suitable to terraces and other small scale farming, plant and animal nutrition and disease control materials, etc. The public sector effort must begin emphasizing the benefits to the private sector of appropriate technology, not replacing private-sector leadership.

b. Participation in the promotion of proper and efficient application of technology. Evidence exists that Yemeni farmers are willing to try and seek out improved production methods. Sometimes the available technology is not suitable to their needs or knowledge of proper use of the machine, plant or material is not available. The public role should be to demonstrate that traders, farmers, marketing firms, commercial banks and other private businesses will all benefit when appropriate technology is efficiently used. Attention should be given to tving the procurement of appropriate technology to its use and servicing.

c. Stimulation of an appreciation of the requirements for gaining access to export markets. The YAR is not likely to become a major exporter of agricultural products; nevertheless, for those products in which it migi.t be able to compete (grapes, certain vegetables) in some market (e.g., Saudi Arabia) a knowledge of such factors as quality requirements, packaging, timing of delivery, etc. is crucial. The public sector should be prepared to play an educational and perhaps regulatory role to help enhance penetration and the long term reputation of Yemeni products in export markets.

d. Utilization of food-aid programs to build local institutions. YARG has recently approached the U.S. Government on the subject of terms for wheat purchases. Among the several possibilties are sales under PL 480, Title I, that provide for application of local currency receipts to self-help programs in the recipient country. One of the institutions crucially needed for the long-term agricultural development of YAR is a faculty of agriculture at Sanaa University. From a development perspective, other considerations aside, Title I funds appear to have a potential for being used in ways consistent with the strategy for development of YAR agriculture.

     e. Adjustment of the import duty structure to help stimulate domestic agricultural production. Higher import duties on food products might be used to attempt to decrease consumption of imports and stimulate demand for domestic products. Aside from the fact that the YARG relies on import duties for revenue, increasing import duties is not likely to accomplish the intended result for the following reasons:

    (1) Food is probably quite inelastic to price changes, so that increasing the import duty and thus retail price would have a minimal effect on the quantity consumed and imported. It would provide a higher price floor for domestic products, but in nearly all cases, imported and local products do not compete directly on price.

    (2) Higher import duties would give greater incentive to smuggling, especially across the open border with Saudi Arabia.

    (3) Even if successful, using duties for the purpose

of influencing consumption patterns would be contrary to YARG policy and will lead to price distortions.

C.   Strategic Considerations

Because of the nature of recent growth in rural incomes, farmers in Yemen do not face very difficult marketing problems. The main issues relate to smoothing out the present flow of food to and from the countryside and guiding public-sector investment into the most appropriate uses. Market intelligence is the most obvious shortcoming in domestic marketing. In 1981, the MAF established a Marketing Department which is the appropriate vehicle for collecting and disseminating relevant price data.

Storage requirements are changing as farmers no longer need to maintain grain reserves for bad years, as they did in the past. On-farm storage techniques and practices are still inadequate and the Marketing Department is again an appropriate agency for extending advice to farmers. Many external donor agencies, multilateral and bilateral, can assist with storage and post-harvest expertise and the MAF should utilize this assistance.

Exporting horticultural produce to Jeddah and other Saudi Arabian markets seems to offer promising prospects. However, these are sophisticated and highly competitive markets, and Yemeni produce must be graded, sorted, cleaned and properly packed before it crosses the border. The establishment of such procedures should be the immediate task of the recently incorporated Agricultural Marketing Corporation, whose exact role at present is unclear. In addition, to ensure proper access to the Saudi Arabian market, close relations would have to be developed with the principal merchants there.

If exploited carefully, exports of fresh produce can rapdily generate more merchandise exports than the traditional exports of coffee, hides and cotton. The rate of growth of exporting fresh produce will ultimately depend on the relative prices of fresh fruits and vegetables in the Yemen and Saudi Arabian markets. In this context, a devaluation of the Yemen riyal would be of prime importance. There would be other effects of such a devaluation, but the impact on exports of fresh produce appears to be the most predictable.

Agro-industrial projects are being promoted for which there appears to have been less than adequate attention paid to their economic viability. With local prices for fresh vegetables, fruit, meat and fish among the highest in the world, there does not appear to be an adequate rationale for promoting processing plants for tomatoes, cotton or fish. The fresh market is always the highest priced, and processing is viable only when supply consistently exceeds demand, which is generally not the case in Yemen.

Physical facilities need continued suppport from both private and public sectors. Clean, hygienic facilities for fish and meat marketing must be expanded in all major market centers. The Hodeidah grain importing facility needs complete renovation. This should be considered in conjunction with the feed and oil complex recommended in this report. Credit must also be made available for private sector initiatives in grain storage facilities and in improving artisanal fishing boats, gear and ice plants.

Price control mechanisms currently operating in Yemen are performing adequately. The free market system is ensuring that prices received by farmers provide them with reasonable profits. Import duties are adequate; in fact, for fresh vegetables, they are probably excessive at 100%.

NOTES

1   At current price ratios, domestically produced grain would not be competitive with imported grain and oil seed prices would probably not be high enough to stimulate local production.

2   IBRD. Report No. 1057a-YAR, May 6, 1976.

3   IBRD. Agricultural Sector Study, November 17, 1981.

4   Liaquat R.S. Jamal, National Cold Storage and Supermarket, personal interview, November 2, 1982.

5   Ministry of Supply and Transport, personal interview, October 31, 1982.

6   IBRD. Report No. 1057a-YAR, Op. cit.

7   Naji A. Awas, Citibank, personal interview, October 6, 1982.

8   IBRD. Agricultural Sector Study, Op. cit.

9   IBRD, Report No. 1057a-YAR and IBRD, Agricultural Sector Study op. cit.

10   Central Bank of Yemen, Financial Statistical Bulletin January-March, 1982, Vol. 10, No. 1. and Naji A. Awas, Citibank, personal interview, October 6, 1982.

11   SFYP, draft copy.

12   Abdul Muamin, Commercial Section Manager, and David Allen, British Agricultural Engineering Advisor, CACB,personal interview, October 26, 1982.

13   It takes an average 5 kgs. of fresh tomatoes to make 1 kg. of paste. The cost of the can and canning usually exceed the cost of purchasing tomatoes. Thus the proposed factory will have to pay at most YR .50 per kg. in order to produce a product that could sell n price alone in the local market.

14   Exceptions: food imports by the GCFT, the Govt. Empl. Soc. and the Military and Police Corp.; distribution of agricultural inputs by CACB.

XIV   THE STRATEGY

A.   Major Changes Affecting Agriculture

This assessment of agriculture in Yemen has examined a number of development constraints and opportunities. There are many areas in which it will be necessary to initiate changes and strengthen performance as the people and government of the YAR continue to grapple with development issues in agriculture. The major events and changes affecting agricultural development that occurred over the past two decades are the following.

1. The opening up during the 1960s of a relatively closed economy which over the past few years has participated actively in the international trade and labor markets.

2. The shift in agriculture from a largely self-contained subsistence farming system to one which, on the demand side, participates broadly in the market economy and, on the supply side, is becoming increasingly market-oriented.

3. The growth of an economy, based largely on the export of labor services, which has

been economically liberal in that it has relied mainly on market forces rather than controls in both the international and domestic markets.

4. The reliance on external sources for the financial and human capital resources necessary to implement public sector development activities.

5. The growth of investment in transportation and communications infrastructure and equipment that has greatly facilitated access by agricultural producers to markets.

6. The shift from a substantial surplus of labor in agriculture to a relatively limited and high-cost labor supply.

7. The increased demand for and investment in water supplies necessary for the vertical intensification of agricultural production and a shift from drought-resistant grain production to other crops.

8. The process of shifting from a risk-adverse agricultural strategy to greater willingness to accept risks in responding to changing consumer demand.

9. The changing of technology and farming

practices required for farm units to adjust to new supply-and-demand conditions.

10. The need for improved and expanded services to support and facilitate the growth of an increasingly complex agricultural investment, production and marketing system, including the demand for trained technical people at all levels.

11. The maintenance of macroeconomic policies which have not discriminated against agriculture. However, the government has apparently made no attempt to form agricultural sector policies which would deal effectively with agricultural development issues.

12. The limited capability of the government to extend its authority throughout the economy on many operating and development matters, because of continuing political dissidence and inadequate institutional capability.

B. Development Issues

Within the above context, there are a number of development issues which will need attention over the next decade, if the agricultural sector is to contribute significantly to the growth of the Yemeni economy.

1. As the amount of officially recorded workers' remittances continues to stagnate, the YARG will need to address policy issues associated with the worsening balance of payments and budgetary situations in ways which stimulate rather than constrain increased agricultural production and marketing.

2. Agricultural sector policies need to be addressed on issues of water utilization, environmental degradation, crop and livestock production alternatives, market potentials, government intervention in the marketing system and the relative roles of the private and public sectors in providing services and access to assets for farmers.

3. Agricultural institutions providing services to farmers need to be strengthened. The MAF needs to increase its capability to plan, monitor and carry out continuing responsibilities and development activities. In so doing, it is essential to improve the data on which policy and investment decisions are based. Of particular importance is increasing the scope and quality of research

and extension services. Moreover, increasing the technical competence and operating effectiveness of departments such as livestock, horticulture, agronomy and irrigation is essential, if the MAF is going to provide relevant services and facilitate changes in farming practices as production and marketing opportunities shift.

4.   Closely related to the above is the requirement to increase human capital resources at all levels in the public and private sectors. The entire range of the education spectrum from basic literacy to the scientific and professional level falls far short of development requirements. Development activities at all levels are constrained: farmers are unable to follow written instructions for utilization of farm inputs; capital is wasted because of the inability to do necessary maintenance and repairs; private investment decisions go wrong because of analytical and planning deficiencies; public and private institutions flounder because trained administrators, scientists, technicians and other support

staff are simply not available; and, development activities financed by donors fail to become institutionalized because counterparts and other Yemeni staff needed on projects are lacking.

5. While farmers have demonstrated a responsiveness to market forces in choosing among production alternatives, their capability to do so in a way which contributes to the expansion of output is limited. Change is inhibited by traditional production patterns which emphasized food security rather than maximizing income from production. Even when farmers are prepared to make changes to produce new crops, a lack of adequate plant materials or seeds, insufficient knowledge at all levels about the performance characteristics of alternative crops, the inability to obtain information on essential cultural practices, the lack of market information and similar constraints severely limit the ability of private-enterprise farmers to adjust to new market conditions.

6. The volume of goods, including agricultural products, supplies and equipment, has

expanded enormously over the past decade. The market has been reasonably effective in handling this increased volume. However, there appear to be two functions of the market which have received inadequate attention. These are the technological appropriateness of imported agricultural inputs and the alternative opportunities for expansion in domestic and international markets.

7. Resource management presents a particular challenge in Yemen. Cultivable land and water for agriculture have always been scarce resources. Labor, which over the centuries has been in surplus in Yemen, is now relatively scarce and certainly high cost per unit. Capital, which in the past depended on surplus labor for creation, is now relatively abundant in agriculture. How to substitute capital for labor in maximizing the effective utilization of the scarce resources, land and labor, will need to be addressed for both the horizontal and vertical expansion of agricultural production. The major problems are maintenancee, enhancement of usable resources and maximizing utilization of existing

resources. This means preventing deterioration of the land while increasing its capacity to retain moisture, improving the effectiveness of water distribution systems and establishing adequate water use management.

C. Other Donor Activities

There are a significant number of areas in which it appears that other donor assistance adequately covers development requirements over the next five years. The highly critical area of agricultural research is being covered by IDA/FAO assistance, supplemented by specialized research financed by bilateral donors as part of project activities. While in undertaking certain projects it may be necessary for a bilateral donor to finance project-specific research, this should only be done in close coordination with CARS.

Livestock investment requirements appear to be adequately covered by European bilateral donors and the private sector, except for increasing the institutional capability of the Livestock Department in the Ministry.

Basic infrastructure supporting agriculture has an adequate flow of investment resources from international and Arab donors, local communities and private enterprise.

While the MAF has planned additional area development projects, the World Bank has strongly recommended that investment during the SFYP period be limited to ongoing projects. Within the context of this recommendation, adequate financing of area development schemes is available.

The World Bank and European bilateral donors are providing assistance for field crops and annual vegetables to determine feasible alternative crops and provide for the distribution of appropriate varieties. However, in the horticultural area the development and distribution of plant material is not being addressed by other donors.

With respect to agricultural education, only graduate study and functional literacy appear to be adequately covered by the donor community.

Fisheries are also receiving necessary support from World Bank and bilateral donors.

D. Strategy Issues

Before setting out the development assistance priorities in agriculture for AID, there are a number of strategy issues which need to be discussed. First, the sector assessment team has been asked to comment on institutional arrangements for carrying out the strategy. A majority of the team believes that the present arrangements with the Consortium for International Development should be continued. While the current system of a collaborative arrangement among CID, the MAF and USAID may not be perfect, there is no guarantee that any other institutional arrangement would provide a contractor able to perform as effectively as CID, given the current CID leadership in the field, the experience of CID in Yemen and the potential professional capacity in the CID member institutions. There are areas in which CID performance needs to be improved. The CID process of selecting lead schools needs to be changed to assure that the school selected has the requisite technical capability. Perhaps some system of peer review could be used. CID also needs to put more stress on language competence. Personnel being posted to Yemen should receive language training up to the S-1, R-1 level and language training should be continued at post. Additionally, care needs to be taken not to overload. New activities or expansion of existing activities should be undertaken only after a determination has been made that CID can provide the necessary assistance. In this connection, CID should be prepared to seek out needed competencies from institutions outside its structure. A continuing dialogue on these and similar issues between CID and USAID within the spirit of Title XII legislation is essential to carrying out successfully the agricultural strategy and program. Given the leadership in USAID and CID, the team believes that a useful dialogue can be maintained.

Second, the team was requested to recommend whether or not AID should continue assistance to the agricultural sector. The team believes such assistance should continue. Agriculture is the most important sector in the domestic economy, both in terms of contribution to GDP and employment. With no known exploitable mineral resources, agriculture must necessarily play the major role in expansion of the domestic production of goods. Expansion of agricultural production will require radical changes in production patterns and the use of agricultural resources. USAID, along with other donors, can play an effective role in helping the Yemenis to make these changes.

Third, the major problem facing USAID in carrying out an effective assistance program in Yemen is implementation rather than strategy, program or design. In order to enhance the image of USAID in Yemen and to better promote program success, it is essential that major attention be focused on implementation. To facilitate this, the assessment team recommends that the number of projects in the agricultural sector be strictly limited. Certainly, given the current number of projects approved, it would not appear appropriate to contemplate initiating more than two or three new projects over the next five years.

Fourth, in selecting projects, great care needs to be taken to avoid undertaking projects which are politically and socially sensitive within the Yemen context.

Fifth, there appears to be a noticeable lack of donor coordination within Yemen. We believe that such coordination would increase the effectiveness of all agricultural projects and programs in Yemen. It would seem appropriate for USAID to foster increased donor coordination under the aegis of the UNDP.

Sixth, it is the conclusion of the assessment team that all projects approved for funding by the USAID, including the CID core project, should be carried out to their planned conclusion. Most, if not all, of the projects are addressing priority concerns identified in this study.

Seventh, activities financed should be selected and designed in a way which recognizes the scarcity of adequately trained counterparts. There are severe problems in having well-qualified counterparts in place in a timely manner, given the shortage of even minimally-trained staff, the competition among donors for counterparts, and the lengthy training periods required to make counterparts effective. Often, counterparts will require initial on-the-job training, then study abroad and, once again, on-the-job training.

E. Strategy Components

Listed below in order of priority are the strategic components proposed for the AID agricultural assistance program in the YAR over the next five years.

1. The first strategic priority is in the area of agricultural education and training. This includes all levels of agricultural education except graduate education and basic literacy, which are being financed within the context of specific projects by a large number of international and bilateral donors including USAID. Education is of the highest priority, because the major impediment to successfully carry out develoment activities is the lack of an effectively functioning staff or work force in the public and private sectors. Within the education area, the top priority must be assigned to B.S. level education. It is these graduates who are needed to staff the scientific, technical and administrative upper levels in public and private institutions and organizations, including the MAF. B.S. level personnel are also desperately needed to direct and implement development projects and provide suitable candidates for advanced degrees. Illustrative of this is the World Bank assisted Agriculture Research and Development Authority project which has a requirement for 44 senior scientists at the technical and administrative level, 49 junior scientists, and 121 technical and administrative staff. While the Bank will provide graduate-level education for most of the senior scientists, no provision is made for B.S. or technical school level education for the junior scientists, technical or administrative staff, or candidates

for advanced degrees. This is not an isolated instance, but representative of staffing and education problems faced by all donor projects and government institutions. While some of the necessary B.S. level education can be provided by training abroad, there is clearly a priority need for continuing agricultural education at the university level in Yemen that merits USAID attention.

Agricultural education for middle level technicians and for skilled personnel such as mechanics and machine operators is important. USAID, the British and the YARG are operating three technical secndary schools, two in agriculture and one in livestock. Other short-term, noninstitutionalized training is being carried out in several projects. However, these education efforts fall far short of meeting demand. Expansion of support for the education of middle level technicians is therefore the second priority for USAID assisvance within the education area. Assistance at the skill level does need better coverage than is being provided by a Bank-assisted literacy project and a British-assisted mechanical agriculture project. However, this high priority need would be more appropriately handled by the Peace Corps than by USAID.

2. The second strategic priority is strengthening the instititional capacity of the MAF and its component parts to carry out its functions. The strategy is directed toward

assisting the MAF to organize and manage its affairs, so
that it may effectively deal with policy, operational and
procedural matters essential to servicing the agricultural
sector. The timing for such assistance in the near future
appears appropriate. The MAF is currently considering reorganization plans, which are expected to be put in place in
the near future. The World Bank is in the process of termin-
ating most of the advisory positions in the MAF that it has
been financing. There is no indication that other donors
are contemplating assistance in this area.

It needs to be recognized that this strategy contem-
plates an expansion of the kinds of assistance being provided to the MAF under the CID Core project. It does not
contemplate initiation of a new activity by USAID, but an
expansion of present involvement with the MAF. It would be
a joint effort to develop the institutional capacity of the
MAF and its general departments to study, plan and carry out
policies and operations. This strategy would not include
assistance to particular general departments for staffing
and implementation of particular programs. For example, it
appears that the reorganization of the MAF will include the
upgrading of extension to a general department and a substantial expansion of extension activities. Under this
strategy, assistance could be provided to the head of
extension in developing plans and procedures for expanding

extension activities, but it would not include a project to develop the extension service. It should be noted in this respect that the World Bank has under preliminary consideration a multi-donor assistance package to develop the Extension Service with FAO. The strategy would also include assistance in developing within the MAF a capability to generate, store, retrieve and use significantly improved data and information. Additionally, it includes the issue of how best to appraise, design and undertake feasibility studies of projects. Both of these functions are critical to the effective functioning of units which would be assisted within the MAF.

3. The third priority is directed toward the effective utilization of the scarce resource, water. Expansion and diversification of agricultural production is dependent on water availability. By and large, other donors, the government or private enterprise. are providing adequate financing for projects to increase the supply of water.

However, little attention is being given to production increases that may be achieved through proper delivery systems and on-farm water management. Observation of current water distribution and utilization practices indicate irrigated areas might be expanded two to three times by improved on-farm water management, once the spate or perenntial flow is brought under control for irrigation. Payoffs occur in the efficient use of water on the farm and in the delivery systems. Because of its importance to the expansion of agricultural production and the conservation of scarce water resources, this area merits consideration for USAID assistance. However, because of the complex social and economic issues in water management and distribution, it is essential that this strategy be implemented by increasing the institutional capability of the MAF to bring aobut needed changes.

4. Fourth priority is given to providing support at local and national levels to development of indigenous private enterprises serving farmers. This might include involvement of the U.S. private sector, most probably as consultants or contractors, rather than as partners in a joint venture. Initially, the area needing to be strengthened is the marketing of farm products and furnishing of farm supplies and equipment to farmers. New markets need to be developed for high-value crops. This will require modern methods of merchandizing, packaging and transporting farm products. On the farm supply side, attention needs to be given to the appropriateness of materials and equipment supplied and the provision of adequate information which will make possible effective use of inputs and a consequent increased demand for them. There may also be some possibility for agro-industry development, either in fabricating

farm equipment, manufacturing farm supplies or processing food products. This is likely to be a longer term potential than is the case with marketing.

5. In concluding this strategy section, the importance of limiting USAID and CID involvement in new agricultural projects over the next five years is once again emphasized. However, better use might be made of various centrally-funded activities, both in support of direct CID-executed programs and in support of relevant projects of other donors. Some specific examples have been cited in this report.

BIBLIOGRAPHY

Adra, Hajwa. Qabyala: The Tribal Concept in the Yemeni Highlands. Ph.D. dissertation, Temple University (Philadelphia), Anthropology, December, 1982.

Asman, Itil. YAR Horticultural Production. Extension and Training. Interim Report. 1982.

Bernhardt, C.F., et al. Water Resources Development Framework for the Yemen Arab Republic. CID, September 1980.

Bornstein, Annika. Food and Society in the Yemen Arab Republic. Rome: FAO, 1974.

_____. "Some Observations on Yemeni Food Habits", FAO Nutrition Newsletter. 10:3 (July-September), 1972.

Bujra, Abdala. The Politics of Stratification. Oxford: Clarendon Press, 1971.

Caroll, P. H. et al. Evaluation, Land Classification and Soil Survey Project Yemen. RONCO Consulting Corp., August, 1982.

CARS. Annual Report, 1930. Taiz.

_____. Annual Report, 1981. Taiz.

_____. Coffee Production and Marketing in the Yemen Arab Republic. 1980.

_____. Crop Damage due to Termites in the Tihama Region, 1981.

_____. Economic Potentials and Imports of Cereals, Fruit and Vegetables. 1981.

_____. Economics of Sorghum Production and Marketing in the Tihama Region. 1982.

_____. Grape Production and Marketing. 1982.

_____. Vegetable Seed Imports, Distribution and Production Possibilities in the Yemen Arab Republic. 1981.

Central Bank of Yemen. Ninth Annual Report. Sanaa, 1980.

_____. _Financial Statistical Bulletin_, Vol 10, No. 1, 1982.

Checchi and Company. _Appropriate Rural Technology for the Yemen Arab Republic_. 1978.

CID. _Agriculture Development Support for the Yemen Arab Republic. Individual Reports_. 1979 (Mimeo)

_____. _Baseline Field Study Report_. Sanaa, 1979.

_____. _Poultry Extension and Training, Revised Subproject Paper_. Sanaa, 1982.

_____. _Subproject Paper for the Horticulture Improvement and Training Subproject (HITS) in the Yemen Arab Republic_. September, 1982.

_____. _Title XII Agricultural Development Support Program. Yemen Arab Republic. Second Annual Work Plan for Core Subproject_. Sanaa, 1982.

_____. FAPU. _Findings and Recommendations as a Result of the Study and Observation Tour by the Faculty of Agriculture Planning United (FAPU)_. Sanaa, October, 1981.

Cohen, J.M. and D.B. Lewis. "Capital Surplus, Labor-short Economics: Yemen as a Challenge to Rural Development Strategies", _American J. of Agricultural Economics_, August, 1977.

_____. _Review of Literature and Analysis of Rural Development Issues in the Yemen Arab Republic_. Ithica: Cornell University, 1979. (Working Note #6).

Cornell University. _Rural Development and Local Organization in Hajja and Hodeidah. Regional Baseline Study Report_. Ithica: Cornell University, Center for Int. Studies, 1980. (2 volumes).

Croken, Barbara. _Source Materials in Arabic on Rural Development and the Cooperative Movement in the Yemen Arab Republic_. Ithica: Cornell University, center for Int. Studies, October, 1980 (Working Note #5).

CYDA. _Work Paper Forwarded by Confederation of Yemeni Cooperatives Development Associations to the Second Yemeni International Development Conference_. (mimeo)

Dewan, H.C. et al. Irrigation Water Quality in the YAR. Taiz: CARS, March, 1978. (UNDP/FAO/Yemen-/73/010)

DHV Consulting Engineers. Wadi Rima Irrigation Development. Amersfort, The Netherlands, 1978.

ECWA. Crop-Sharing and Land Tenancy Practices in the Yemen Arab Republic. Report No. 1. July, 1980.

FAO. Training and Demonstration in Food Loss Assessment and Prevention of On-Farm Storage Losses. 1982.

Gerholm, Tomas. Market, Mosque and Mafraj. Stockholm: University of Stockholm, 1977.

Ghaleb, Mohammed Anam. Government Organization as a Basis to Economic Development in Yemen. Bochum, Germany: Institute for Development Research on Development Problems, Ruhr University, 1979.

Gibb, Sir Alexander and Partners. Development of Wadi Bana. Stage I, Preliminary Report. June, 1977.

Green, James W. Local Initiative in Yemen: Exploratory Studies of Four Local Development Associations. USAID, 1975.

Hakrow, Sir William and Partners. Wadi Surdud Development. London, 1978. (four volumes.)

Hebert, Mary. Local Organization and Development. Maghlaf, Hodeidah Governorate. Cornell University, Center for Int. Studies, June, 1981. (Working Note #10).

Hendrikson Associates. Final Implementation Plan and Operation Programme, 1978-1981. 1981

_____. Livestock Credit and Processing Project YAR. Program Report No. 16 July 1 - September 30, 1980. 1980.

_____. Review of Livestock Finishing Division. 1981.

Hodson, J., Broadnax, M., Krezdorn, A. H. Evaluation, Tropical and Sub-Tropical Fruit Project. Yemen RONCO Consulting Corp. Report, July 1981.

IBRD. Agricultural Sector Study. November, 1981.

_____. Appraisal of a Grain Storage and Processing Project, Yemen Arab Republic. May 6, 1976. (#1057a - YAR)

_____. Management Development in the Yemen Arab Republic. March 27, 1981.

International Monetary Fund. Yemen Arab Republic. Staff Report for the 1982 Article IV Consultation. June 17, 1982 (SM 82/118).

Italconsul. Sanaa Basin Groundwater Studies Water Supply for Sanaa and Hodeidah, Yemen Arab Republic. Rome: WHO, May, 1973. (three volumes)

Jaycox, E.R. Ibb Secondary Agricultural Institute. Sub-Project TDY Report. March 29-April 29, 1982. CID, 1982.

Johnson, R.J. Water Resources Planning and Development Policy Recommendations, May, 1982.

Kanoon, Adil, et al. Mobilization of Domestic Financial Resources in the Yemen Arab Republic. Washington, D.C.: World Bank, 1982.

Maktari, Abdullah. Water Rights and Irrigation Practices in Lahj. Cambridge: Cambridge Univ. Press, 1971

Merabet, Zohra. A Survey on Development and Management of Water Resources in the Yemen Arab Republic. Sanaa, May, 1980.

_____. A Survey of Water Activities Under Foreign Assistance in the YAR. Sanaa, October, 1980.

Ministry of Overseas Development. Yemen Arab Republic Montane Plain and Wadi Rima Project. Great Britain, 1977.

Mohindra, M.K. Agricultural Research and Institutional Support. Yem/78/009, May, 1982. (End of assignment report).

_____. Benefits from Use of Irrigation in Vineyards of YAR. Taiz: CARS November, 1981.

El Mubasher, Mustafa. Study of the Possiblities of Substituting the Imported Agricultural Foodstuffs by Domestic Production in the Yemen Arab Republic. N.D. (mimeo).

al-Mujahid, Muhammad. Al-Ta^{c}awun al-Zira^{c}i madkhal lil-Tanmiya fi al-Jumhuria al-^{c}Arabiya al-Yeamaniya. Cairo: Dar al-Hana, 1978.

Mundy, Martha. "Woman's Inheritance of Land in Highland Yemen," Arabian Studies, Vol. V, pp.   , 1979.

Myntti, Cynthia. Women and Development in Yemen Arab Republic. Eschborn: GTZ, 1979.

Nyrop, Richard F. et al. Area Handbook for the Yemens. Washington, D.C.: U.S. Govt. Printing Office, 1977.

ODA. A Comparison of Five USA, Two Kenyan and Local (Roumi) Maize Under Irrigation on the Montane Plains. DAIC, Publication #31, 1982.

_____. A Comparison of Introduced and Local Varieties of Wheat and Barley on a Rainfed Terrace. DAIC, Publication #37, 1982.

_____. A Comparison of Nine Introduced and Two Local Varieties of Alflalfa Grown Under Irrigation on the Montane Plains. DAIC, Publication #20, 1981.

_____. The Effect of Five Irrigation Frequencies on Sonalike Wheat (Summer 1981). DAIC, Publication #35, 1982.

_____. Rainfall on the Montane Plains 1975-1980. DAIC, Publication #14, 1981.

_____. Report for April-June 1982 of the Dahmar Agricultural and Forestry Research and Development Project.

_____. The Response to Nitrogen of a Perennial/Italian Tetraploid Ryegrass Mixture Grown under Irrigation. DAIC, Publication #22, 1981.

_____. Summary of Maize (Grain) Trials 1978-1980. DAIC, Publication #4, 1980.

_____. Summary of Sorghum (Grain) Trials 1978-1980.
    DAIC, Publication #3, 1980.

Ross, Lee Ann. An Informal Banking System. The
    Remittance Agent of Yemen. Ithica: Cornell
    University, 1981.

Serjeant, R.B. "Cereal Cultivation in Medieval Yemen,"
    Arabian Studies Vol. I, pp. 25-181, 1974.

Siddiqui, D.A. and S. Ghawi. Human Resources Needs
    Assessment Survey in the Yemen Arab Republic for the
    Second Five-Year Plan Period. Sanaa: CPO, 1981.

Steffen, Hans et al. Final Report on the Airphoto
    Interpretation Project of the Swiss Technical
    Co-Operation Service. Zurich, April, 1978.

Stevenson, Thomas B. Agricultural Extension Services in
    Yemen: Assessment of Current Programs and
    Recomendations for Improvement. Sanaa: C.I.D., July
    16, 1982.

Swanson, Jon. Emigration and Economic Development; The
    Case of the Yemen Arab Republic. Boulder, Colorado:
    Westview Press, 1979.

_____. Draft Report on Beni Awwam. (Unpublished).

Taha, M.A. and A.M. Banaga. Faculty of Agriculture.
    University of Sanaa. Yemen Arab Republic. FAO, 1982.
    (TCP/YEM/0104).

Tesco-Viziterv-Vituki. Survey of the Agricultural
    Potential of the Wadi Zabid. Budapest, 1971.
    (numerous volumes).

Tipton and Kalmbach, Inc. Development of Wadi Mawr.
    Denver, 1979.

Tutwiler, Richard and Sheila Carapico. Yemeni Agriculture
    and Economic Change. Sanaa: AIYS, 1981.

UNDP. Development Cooperation Report for the Year 1981.
    Yemen Arab Republic. Sanaa, 1982.

_____. Summary of International Assistance to the Yemen
    Arab Republic in 1981. Sanaa, 1981.

USAID. Draft AID Policy Paper. Women in Development. Washington, D.C. 1982. (Draft Copy)

_____. Pricing, Subsidies, and Related Policies in Food and Agriculture. AID Policy Paper. 1982. (Draft copy)

Varisco, Daniel Martin. The Adaptive Dynamics of Water Allocation in al-Ahjur, Yemen Arab Republic. Ph.D. Thesis, University of Pennsylvania (Philadelphia), Anthropology, December, 1982.

_____. "The Ard in Highland Yemeni Agriculture," Tools and Tillage (Denmark), Winter, 1982.

_____. "The Meaning of Chewing: The Significance of Qat in the Yemen Arab Republic." Paper presented at the Annual Meeting of the M.E.S.A., Philadelphia, November, 1982.

_____. "Affluence and the Concept of the Tribe in the Central Highlands of the Yemen Arab Republic." Proceedings of the American Ethnological Society for 1981. (in press).

World Bank. Development of a Traditional Economy. Yemen Arab Republic. Washington, D.C. January 1979.

_____. Effects of Migration of Rural Labor on Agricultural Development. Washington, D.C. 1979.

_____. Mobilization of Domestic Financial Resources in the Yemen Arab Republic. Washington, D.C., January 6, 1982.

_____. Report and Recommendations of the International Development Association to the Executive Director on a Prepared Credit to the Yemen Arab Republic for an Agricultural Research and Development Project. Washington, D.C., 1981.

_____. Report and Recommendations of the President of the International Development Association to the Executive Director on a Proposed Credit in an Amount Equivalent to US $5.5 Million to the Yemen Arab Republic for an Agricultural Credit Project. (mimeo)

_____. Second Five-Year Plan for the General Directorate of Irrigation (1982-1986). September, 1981. (prepared by Bank mission).

_____. Yemen Arab Republic. Agricultural Research and
Development Project. Staff Appraisal Report.
Washington, D.C., May 7, 1982.

_____. Yemen Arab Republic Economic Memorandum.
Washington, D.C., October 23, 1980.

_____. Yemen Arab Republic. Fisheries Development
Project. Staff Appraisal Report. Washington, D.C.,
April 15, 1980.

Wyckoff, J.B. et. al. Agricultural Sector Analysis.
Yemen Arab Republic. CID, October, 1981.

Yemen Arab Republic. CPO. The First Five-Year Plan
1976/77-1980/81. Sanaa, 1977.

_____. CPO. Second Five-Year Plan, Sanaa, 1982 (English
draft)

_____. CPO. Statistical Year Book 1981. Sanaa, April,
1982.

_____. MAF. A Foreign Trade Publication on Agricultural
Materials and Supplies, 1971-1980. Sanaa, January,
1982.

_____. MAF. Summary of the Final Results of the
Agricultural Census in Six Provinces. June, 1981.

_____. MAF. Department of Plant Protection. Plant
Protection Bulletin (Sanaa), Vol. 003/82, 1982.

_____. Ministry of Supply. Yemen Arab Republic National
Nutrition Survey 1979.